Hamlet

Open Guides to Literature

Series Editor: Graham Martin (Professor of Literature,
The Open University)

Titles in the Series

Angus Calder: Byron
Jenni Calder: *Animal Farm* and *1984*
Walford Davies: Dylan Thomas
Roger Day: Larkin
Peter Faulkner: Yeats: *The Tower* and *The Winding Stair*
P. N. Furbank: Pound
Graham Holderness: *Hamlet*
Graham Holderness: *Women in Love*
Graham Holderness: *Wuthering Heights*
Jeannette King: *Jane Eyre*
Graham Martin: *Great Expectations*
Dennis Walder: Hughes
Roderick Watson: MacDiarmid

GRAHAM HOLDERNESS

Hamlet

Open University Press
Milton Keynes · Philadelphia

Open University Press
Open University Educational Enterprises Limited
12 Cofferidge Close
Stony Stratford
Milton Keynes MK11 1BY, England

and
242 Cherry Street
Philadelphia, PA 19106, USA

First Published 1987

British Library Cataloguing in Publication Data
Holderness, Graham
    Hamlet. — (Open guides to literature).
    1. Shakespeare, William. Hamlet
    I. Title
    822.3'7   PR2807

ISBN 0 335 15268 6

ISBN 0 335 15267 8 Pbk

Library of Congress Cataloging in Publication Data
Holderness, Graham.
    Hamlet. (Open guides to literatrue)
    Bibliography: p.
    Includes index.
    1. Shakespeare, William, 1564–1616. Hamlet.
I. Shakespeare, William, 1564–1616. Hamlet.   II. Title.
III. Series.
PR2807.H565 1988   822.3'3   87–7296

ISBN 0–335–15268–6

ISBN 0–335–15267–8 (pbk.)

Project Management: Clarke Williams
Printed in Great Britain

for Marilyn, Tamsyn and Rachel

Contents

Series Editor's Preface

The intention of this series is to provide short introductory books about major writers, texts, and literary concepts for students of courses in Higher Education which substantially or wholly involve the study of Literature.

The series adopts a pedagogic approach and style similar to that of Open University Material for Literature courses. *Open Guides* aim to inculcate the reading 'skills' which many introductory books in the field tend, mistakenly, to assume that the reader already possesses. They are, in this sense, 'teacherly' texts, planned and written in a manner which will develop in the reader the confidence to undertake further independent study of the topic. They are 'open' in two senses. First, they offer a three-way tutorial exchange between the writer of the *Guide*, the text or texts in question, and the reader. They invite readers to join in an exploratory discussion of texts, concentrating on their key aspects and on the main problems which readers, coming to the texts for the first time, are likely to encounter. The flow of a *Guide* 'discourse' is established by putting questions for the reader to follow up in a tentative and searching spirit, guided by the writer's comments, but not dominated by an over-arching and single-mindedly-pursued argument or evaluation, which itself requires to be 'read'.

Guides are also 'open' in a second sense. They assume that literary texts are 'plural', that there is no end to interpretation, and that it is for the reader to undertake the pleasurable task of discovering meaning and value in such texts. *Guides* seek to provide, in compact form, such relevant biographical, historical and cultural information as bears upon the reading of the text, and they point the reader to a selection of the best available critical discussions of it. They are not in themselves concerned to propose, or to counter, particular readings of the texts, but rather to put *Guide* readers in a position to do that for themselves. Experienced travellers learn to dispense with guides, and so it should be for readers of this series.

There are many different texts of *Hamlet* available — Further Reading will give you a brief 'consumer guide' to them — but the text recommended for use with this *Open Guide* is the *New Cambridge Shakespeare* edition, edited by Philip Edwards (Cambridge University Press, 1985). My particular references to act, scene and line of the play (e.g. 1.2.35–40 – Act One, scene 2, lines 35–40) are to this edition; but provided that you are aware of the variations between different texts (discussed below), and are prepared to search a scene for a specific context under discussion, there is no reason why you shouldn't use whatever text of the play you may have to hand.

Acknowledgements

For permission to reproduce illustrations, I am grateful to Wight Collins Rutherford Scott, the Tate Gallery, London, the Shakespeare Birthplace Trust and Joe Cocks Studio, Stratford-upon-Avon, City of Birmingham Public Libraries Department, and the Bibliotheek der Rijkuniversiteit, Utrecht.

Debts of gratitude are due to John Turner, echoes of whose work on *Hamlet* will be found at many points in this book; to Christopher J. McCullough, who worked with me on aspects of *Hamlet* in performance; and to the students of the University College of Swansea Department of Adult Educations's Literature Foundation course, 1985–6, for their help in clarifying and formulating the book's methods and ideas.

LIST OF ILLUSTRATIONS

1. History and Myth

I will assume from the outset that you have read the play through once and are familiar with the shape of its action and the broad outlines of its dramatic structure – that is, with the ordered line of the story and the arrangement and juxtaposition of events and scenes. Chapter Three will involve a more detailed study of Acts 1 and 2 of the play; Chapter Four will dwell on Act 3; and Chapter Five will assume a closer knowledge of Acts 4 and 5. So please read through the whole of the play once before starting on the discussion that follows. Don't spend a long time trying to work our 'motivation' and 'character', or puzzling over difficult and obscure pieces of verse: take the movement and sweep of the action in your stride as if you were watching the play in a theatre.

I

Hamlet is the best-known work of Britain's most famous writer. As such the play occupies a distinctive position within British culture, and exists in forms that lie outside the institutions of theatre and education which are its natural home. Just as the name of Shakespeare is such a common property that it can be invoked in advertisements, television comedies, beer-mats and many other contexts of everyday experience: so the figure of Hamlet, the black-costumed character with the pale face, the skull and the well-worn catch-phrases – 'To be or not to be, that is the question'; 'Alas, poor Yorick! I knew him well' – can appear with instant recognisability in stand-up comedy routines, irreverent parodies, or television adverts. *Hamlet* evidently drew on a popular dramatic tradition, since there was at least one other play of the same name well-known on the Elizabethan stage before Shakespeare's play appeared. When it did appear it was a very popular play in its own right; and the impetus of that popularity was sustained for hundreds of years. Charles Dickens in *Great Expectations* (1861) described with memorable comic verve a Victorian performance before a popular audience which seems to have attended with a pantomime-like vigour of participation:

> The late king of the country … carried a ghostly manuscript round its truncheon, to which it has the appearance of occasionally referring, and that, too, with an air of anxiety and a tendency to lose the place of reference which were suggestive of a state of mortality. It was this, I conceive, which led to the Shade's being advised by the gallery to 'turn over!' – a recommendation which it took extremely ill.
>
> … Whenever [Hamlet], that undecided Prince had to ask a question or state a doubt, the public helped him out with it. As for example; on the question whether 'twas nobler in the mind to suffer, some roared yes, and some no, and some inclining to both opinions said 'toss up for it' …[1]

More recently a television advertisement for Carling Black Label beer (see illustration 1) shows an actor playing Hamlet extricate himself from the embarrassment of dropping Yorick's skull, by exercising the miraculous skills of ball-control admired in professional footballers. Both these examples testify to the continuing intelligibility of *Hamlet*, and to the survival of Shakespeare's play as a ground on which a satirical interaction of 'high' and 'low' cultures can be joined. Both instances are of course irreverent and subversive: but there can be no irreverence without reverence, and no subversion without an established structure to overturn. Shakespeare's *Hamlet* is therefore part of the common currency of our culture, and possesses meanings and values which cannot be contained by its existence as a literary text for study, or a theatrical script for occasional dramatic revival.

Still less can those meanings, values and associations be regarded as circumscribed by the direct control of an 'author'. Some recent literary theory has questioned the very concept of authorship, pointing out that our culture invests enormous significance in the idea of the individual author as the creative and controlling force behind literary works, despite the fact that they are self-evidently constructed from all sorts of linguistic, conventional, and ideological materials which exist quite beyond the scope of the author's imagination and are certainly not in any sense under

1   *Popular Hamlet*

the author's control. It can be plausibly argued with reference to
modern conditions of authorship that it is still the individual writer
who gives final shape to the work, and that it is that individual and
distinctive form that distinguishes literature as 'art' from other
kinds of communication, language and ideological formation. In
the case of Shakespeare, or indeed of any Renaissance dramatist,
this case is much harder to prove: as we shall see in more detail
below, a work like *Hamlet* seems never to have been within the
complete control of the 'author' William Shakespeare. His own
'writing' of it took the form of a dramatic script, which was used as
a basis for the collaborative process of theatrical production rather
than for publication as the work of an individual writer's creative
productivity. *Hamlet* was printed in Shakespeare's lifetime, but in
at least two very different forms, and the text which formed the
basis for most subsequent editions, the First Folio of 1623, was

compiled after Shakespeare's death. The modern edited text you are using now is the accumulated product of centuries of editorial and scholarly work, all dedicated to establishing the authentic utterance of the individual artist: but all executed entirely without Shakespeare's knowledge or permission.

Many people would dispute this view that the concept of authorship is itself a kind of cultural myth. Few people on the other hand would deny that the status of Shakespeare within British culture, like that of all 'national' writers, constitutes some kind of mythological phenomenon. Like all myths, the image of Shakespeare exists in a contradictory synthesis of consensus and plurality. While it is tacitly assumed that 'Shakespeare' means any one of a number of things – great art, the English national spirit, transcendent wisdom, moral profundity, political insight, historical truth, etc. – the diverse and variant forms in which people express and argue these values makes nonsense of any self-contained and coherent totality of conditions and qualities that could usefully be labelled 'Shakespeare'. 'Universality' consists not in the capacity to maintain a fixed and immutable form, but in the ability to be interpreted, appropriated, mobilised in the service of many different views, purposes and ideologies.

In the same way, when we consider that Shakespeare's play *Hamlet* exists in a strange variety of different forms, we become more aware that the meanings, associations and values embodied in the images of the play that operate within our culture need to be traced not only to the theatrical work of a dramatist working on the early Jacobean stages, but also to the accreted meanings bestowed on that play by subsequent cultures and by other societies. What *Hamlet* meant and means in the eighteenth, nineteenth and twentieth centuries clearly has some complex relationship with the script originally written by William Shakespeare, and with the play produced on the London stage not long after 1600: but in each case the meanings are very obviously also a product of the particular historical and cultural circumstances of their time. Peter Hall once attempted to define the play's mythical quality in this way:

> *Hamlet* is one of mankind's great images. It turns a new face to each century, even to each decade. It is a mirror which gives back the reflection of the age that is contemplating it. And the need to define these reflections produces, on average, a new appreciation of *Hamlet* every twelve years.[2]

Thus the play *Hamlet* can be simultaneously a part of history and something immediately contemporary to every generation: its capacity for change is regarded as equally characteristic with its immanent permanence of form. The contradictions evident in Hall's argument are visible in his metaphor – the play is both a mirror and the image that mirror reflects. But if a 'new appreciation' is a new image, how can we think of the mirror as remaining unchanged? The contradictions are not merely evidence of sloppy thinking. The paradox of universality and historical particularity, of an entity which survives by lending itself to constant radical re-interpretation, a play which is always the same yet always different – belongs to the very nature of literature, and stands at the centre of one of literary criticism's most intractable critical and theoretical problems. It is a problem that will not be resolved by our study of *Hamlet*, but a continual awareness of its existence may render that study a richer, more complex and more 'open' process.

II

If we ask what particular conditions have made *Hamlet* itself such a 'survivor', the problem becomes at once more particular and more general. The story from which the play derives its plot is one of great antiquity, dating back beyond the twelfth century to a period when story and myth were one and the same, and to cultural conditions in which such stories were the common property of a people. The story of Amleth can be found in Saxo Grammaticus' Latin history of Denmark *Historica Danicae*, printed in 1514:[3] it contains the basic structure of Shakespeare's dramatic action. Amleth's father, who had defeated the king of Norway in a duel, is murdered by his brother Feng, who then marries the widow Gerutha. Amleth feigns madness to avert suspicion: he is tested for sanity by having a 'fair woman' placed in his way. He kills an eavesdropping friend of Feng's and harangues his mother for marrying her husband's murderer. He is sent to Britain with two companions who carry a secret letter to the British king demanding Amleth's death, and he turns the tables on them by altering the letter to an instruction for their execution. He returns to Denmark and exacts his revenge by killing Feng. He convinces the people that his conduct has been appropriate and that he is the rightful king: they accept him as their ruler.

Compare this summary of the original story with the action of Shakespeare's play, and consider the following questions.

  (i)   How closely do the two narratives correspond?
 (ii)   What substantial difference can you see between the two?
(iii)   Is there anything of importance in Shakespeare evidently missing from
        the old story?

DISCUSSION

(i) As you can see, the old story exhibits sources for old
Hamlet's defeat of old Norway (1.1.84–95), Claudius' murder of
old Hamlet and marriage to Gertrude, Hamlet's feigned madness,
the plot to use Ophelia (3.1), the scene in which Hamlet upbraids
his mother and the killing of Polonius (3.4), the conspiracy of
Rosencrantz and Guildenstern (narrated in 5.2), and the
completion of Hamlet's revenge by the death of Claudius.

(ii) The old saga version is a success story, since Amleth's
revenge results in his acceding to the throne. Shakespeare's
treatment is a tragedy in which the protagonist perishes at the
precise moment of his fulfilling his revenge. The kingdom Hamlet
regards as rightfully his inheritance reverts to Norway, and old
Hamlet's work is undone as his ghost is appeased.

(iii) Surely the most obvious missing element is the ghost itself.
In the old story the murdered father does not reappear to enjoin on
his son the obligation of revenge.

In the Elizabethan dramatic versions the ghost seems to have
been particularly emphasised – it is for example the detail Thomas
Lodge in 1596 recalled and recorded from the pre-Shakespearean
play of Hamlet: 'the ghost who cried so miserally [sic] at the
Theatre like an oyster-wife, "Hamlet, revenge!"'[4] But this
significant contrast seems to lie not in divergent approaches to the
supernatural, but in changing attitudes to revenge. Consider two
passages from earlier versions of the Hamlet story: the first is from
Saxo Grammaticus, the second from the French version which the
Elizabethan playwrights used as a direct source, Francoise de
Belleforest's *Histoire Tragiques* (1570), quoted here from the
anonymous English translation of 1608:

(1)   O valiant Amleth, and worthy of immortal fame, who being
shrewdly armed with a feint of folly, covered a wisdom too high
for human wit under a marvellous disguise of silliness! and not
only found in his subtlety means to protect his own safety, but
also by its guidance found opportunity to avenge his father. By
this skilful defence of himself, and strenuous revenge for his

parent, he has left it doubtful whether we are to think more of his wit or his bravery.

(2)   If vengeance ever seemed to have any show of justice, it is then, when pietie and affection constraineth us to remember our fathers unjustly murdered, as the things wherby we are dispensed withal, and which seek the means not to leave treason and murther unpunished ... where the prince or country is interested, the desire of revenge cannot by any meanes (how small soever) beare the title of condemnation, but is rather commendable and worthy of praise.[5]

What difference can you detect in their views of revenge?

DISCUSSION

In the old saga story there is nothing morally problematical about revenge: while Belleforest found it necessary to reassure his readers that in the particular circumstances of this story revenge could be justified. There needs no ghost come from the grave to instruct 'Amleth' in a duty which. no-one in twelfth-century Denmark would have dreamed of questioning. Far from being regarded as a crime, revenge was built into the legal systems and moral conventions of those early societies in such a way that moral obligation on Amleth's part can simply be assumed. By the sixteenth century such justification was needed because revenge as a judicial institution had disappeared with the old tribal and feudal laws, and was regarded in new-style Christian national monarchies like France and England as a crime and a sin by legal authorities and by the church. Thus the dramatists of Shakespeare's time perhaps needed to insert some compelling and powerful incentive to vengence into their plays to fill this gap between the morality of the old tale and the ethics of contemporary society.

We will be examining the moral problems of revenge in more detail in Chapter 3. As we have seen, *Hamlet* originated in a form of popular story; and it belongs to a form of dramatic entertainment extremely popular in its own day, that of the revenge tragedy. The revenge pattern as a narrative and dramatic structure for works of art seems to have obdurate and persistent vitality, quite independent of the moral codes of the societies in which such works appear. Personal revenge is forbidden by the morality of our own society, and as an individual passion it can hardly be said to play an important role in our social life. Yet many of our cultural forms (westerns and soap operas, to give only two examples) use the revenge convention as a basic framework for their actions: offering fictional stories of poetic justice as narrative resolutions of problems which would be much more intractable if dealt with by processes of law. People will often affirm that revenge is a basic human instinct; and it is certainly a deeply-felt moral obligation in societies where family and kinship loyalties entail defending the security or honour of the group by punitive or deterrent revenge against aggression or insult. But revenge is very different from an immediate impulse of passionate reprisal; it is deliberate, premeditated and based on a sense of justice. In a society which accepts revenge as a judicial institution, the forms of its execution are always very elaborate and necessarily very public.

It is difficult to see why revenge should be regarded as more innate in human beings than the desire to refer intractable moral problems to a state which can justly claim to guarantee justice and equity to all parties. We think of a passionate act of revenge as an instinct, and a High Court hearing as an impersonal institution: but it is our human nature that has made both as attempts to achieve justice.

III

Hamlet belongs then to an old type of popular story, and to a popular form of fiction with an extraordinary vitality and persistence. Yet neither of these factors can really explain the *kind* of familiarity the play enjoys in our contemporary culture, since that familiarity is always associated with Shakespeare, with the Elizabethan theatre or the establishment theatre of our own day, and with particular notions of 'high culture' bound up in all these elements. It is Shakespeare's Hamlet we recognise, not Saxo's or Belleforest's. when Mel Brooks in his recent remake of the Ernst Lubitsch comedy *To Be or Not to Be*[6] appears on a stage reciting the famous soliloquy, we know it is a 'Shakespearean' performance that is being parodied and subverted. When a comedian appears in a black doublet and tights holding a skull, we know the object of mockery is Shakespearean theatre.

Many of Shakespeare's plays exist in this popular dimension in the form of a single compelling image which is offered as a crystallisation of the essence of the whole play. Richard III calling for a horse, Othello strangling Desdemona, King Lear on the blasted heath, are all archetypal cultural symbols with a strong tradition of visual representation behind their familiarity. We all know *Romeo and Juliet* through the famous 'balcony scene', which is represented together with a statue of Shakespeare on the British £20 note: all the play's well-known catch-phrases ('Romeo, Romeo, wherefore art thou Romeo', 'a rose by any other name', 'parting is such sweet sorrow') come from that one scene. The play *Hamlet* has been similarly universalised in the form of a single image – that of the black-clothed prince holding a skull.

I would like you now to consider this image and to examine some of its representations; to explore some of the meanings and associations attached to it, and to consider what implications these have for our study of the play. The image occurs in the play not (as many representations have understandably though erroneously suggested) together with Hamlet's 'To be or not to be' soliloquy, but in the 'graveyard scene' before Ophelia's funeral. It might be a good idea for you to read that passage (5.1.1–183) before undertaking the following exercises.

First of all, look at three representations of this image: illustrations 2–4 (pp. 10–12). Illustration 2 shows the great actor of the Romantic period, John Philip Kemble, who played the role from 1783 to 1817; illustration 3 shows Ben Kingsley in Buzz Goodbody's 1975 production at Stratford's studio theatre, the Other Place; and illustration 4 is a statue of Hamlet which stands in an Avonside park by the Royal Shakespeare Theatre.[7]

> Examine each in turn, and note down anything that strikes you about each one. Everyone has an image of what Hamlet should look like. Which of these pictures approximates most accurately to your own conceptions?

Most people would probably feel that the statue represents Hamlet most accurately: partly because of the Elizabethan costume, and partly because the figure's pose (it recalls Rodin's *Thinker*) shows the prince bowed with the gravity of deep philosophical thought. Kemble's Hamlet would perhaps come next in order of proximity to our concept of an appropriate image: the isolated melancholy figure, gazing into space, grasping the skull but looking beyond it towards the greater mysteries of life and death. Ben Kingsley's presentation of the role is clearly designed to clash against more traditional images: the actor looks more like a ventriloquist with his dummy than the noble melancholy intellectual of the romantic tradition. The scruffy overcoat obtrusively affirms an uncompromising 'modernity' of dress.

2   *Kemble as Hamlet*

DISCUSSION

Whichever version you preferred (and the results of such an
exercise may well vary widely according to individual experience)
most people would probably regard the first two Hamlets as
'traditional' in style and the last as avant-garde or 'modern'. But it

3 *Ben Kingsley as Hamlet*

is important to be exact about the origins of a tradition. Do we mean that some images of Hamlet display a direct continuity with the original Jacobean production, and are therefore more authentically in line with the author's intended meaning than others? If so, then these images are quite misleading. As we shall see in more detail below, what we think of as 'traditional' or 'historical' costume was not used in the theatre before the nineteenth century, and was established as part of a general attempt

4   *Statuesque Hamlet*

to reconstruct and reproduce Elizabethan staging conditions. Prior to these innovations theatrical costume was based, as it was in the Elizabethan theatres, on the contemporary dress of the day. (See illustration 5, a representation of *Hamlet* from the early eighteenth century, where despite historical touches like Gertrude's ruff, the costume clearly suggests contemporary rather than Elizabethan style.)[8] It could therefore be suggested that a modern-dress Hamlet

5   *Hamlet of 1709*

is a more authentic bearer of the Elizabethan tradition than a
Hamlet in Elizabethan costume.

There are other ways in which our conception of Hamlet can be
a nineteenth-century rather than an Elizabethan conception.
Shakespeare's Hamlet was played by his company's leading
tragedian Richard Burbage, a mature and very heavy actor in his
late 30s – it has been suggested that Gertrude's line 'He's fat and

scant of breath' (5.2.264) was a joke at Burbage's expense. When Nicol Williamson – a large and burly man – played Hamlet in 1969 (and in Tony Richardson's 1970 film), his performance seemed a radical break with tradition: yet in a sense the role was being returned to the physical style of its original performance.[9] Those actors who in the late eighteenth and early nineteenth centuries formulated the romantic image of Hamlet represented in Sir Thomas Lawrence's portrait of Kemble, were establishing a very modern and contemporary style which would later be confused with an authentic and historical Elizabethan manner of presentation. Kemble is said to have devised a costume for the role based on seventeenth century pictures by Van Dyke: yet the costume in the portrait looks, with the cloak and open-necked shirt, irresistibly suggestive of Lord Byron (one of whose posturings was, incidentally, to drink wine out of a skull).

If we try to evaluate these different images in terms of their accuracy and fidelity to Shakespeare's text, we will find only ambivalence and complexity. Unlike the naturalistic plays of the later nineteenth century, such as those of Shaw or Ibsen, which provide enormous amounts of information about how the authors wanted the plays performed, Renaissance play-texts are short on stage directions, and the only other hints we are given take the form of internal references to costume or appearance. Thus we know that the ghost wears armour, or that Osric wears a bonnet, from references within the text. Such details give little assistance to the reader or theatrical director seeking an appropriate visual style. The romantic images of Hamlet holding the skull correspond accurately enough to the prince's vein of philosophical meditation. On the other hand the graveyard scene (5.1) is a comic scene, the skull is that of a jester, and Hamlet's observations on it appear (to our perceptions if not to the more robust sensibilities of the Elizabethans) to be a string of sick jokes: so we might feel that Ben Kingsley's death's-head grin is actually a more accurate articulation of the scene than the romantic images.

The important conclusion to draw here from these illustrations is that our images of Hamlet are never innocent or spontaneous: they do not simply arise from the individual reader's response to the play. They derive from somewhere, even though a direct transmission may be hard to prove. When the text of a Renaissance play is simply *read*, we convert it into a kind of novel. Yet the text contains only one element of the narrative completeness we could expect from a novel: speech. The very few formal stage directions, and the larger number of internal stage directions, cannot possibly supply all the descriptive details of concrete social situation, visual appearance, tones of voice, that we would expect a realistic novel to supply. So we supply imaginatively all these missing elements: we *must* visualise Hamlet, Claudius, Ophelia: we *must* imagine the battlements of Elsinore or the Danish court, if we are to read the play at all. A theatrical performance, which also has to fill in the blanks in the bare text, would correspond more closely in this respect to a novel: but a dramatic script like a Shakespeare play can only be made into a text-for-performance by converting it into what in the theatre is called a 'prompt-book' — in which the verbal skeleton is fleshed with specific directions about acting, blocking, mise-en-scène, lighting, music, etc.

Readers often claim a complete liberty of the imagination: you might well protest that your reading of *Hamlet* is your own personal 'production', and not derived from elsewhere. I can only ask you to examine the various representations of the play provided in this guide, to test whether or not my contention is true. When I read *Hamlet* as an 'A' level student my visual images of the characters and the locations were very distinct, and so far as I knew my own imaginative invention. I later discover that they were identical to Laurence Olivier's 1948 film version,[10] which I had never seen. What I *had* seen was an amateur performance which imitated the Olivier version with a perverse and perfect accuracy; and I had taken part in a school production also heavily influenced by the film.[11] Olivier's performance consolidated and popularised the romantic image of the prince: and that became, through a complex process of cultural transmission, my image. We need therefore, not only to study the text of the play, but to be aware of the spaces that text leaves in the action, and how these various different representations have occupied those spaces.

We can now look more closely at the kinds of meaning, association and value attached to this paradigmatic image of the play. The portrait of Kemble (illustration 2) was painted by Sir Thomas Lawrence for the Royal Academy in 1801. It was bought by W. A. Madocks, a philanthropic entrepreneur who built the model town of Tremadoc in North Wales, one of the age's 'utopian socialist' attempts to build an ideal industrial community. Madocks intended to use the portrait as an altar-piece in the church, where one would normally expect to find a representation of Christ: but permission for this was refused by the local diocesan bishop.

(i) What does this incident tell us about the particular image of Hamlet?
(ii) Look again at illustration 4. Notice that the skull is miraculously free from the coating of verdigris which invests the bronze figure. Can you imagine why that should be so?

(i) Madocks seems to have wanted to use the image of Hamlet as an icon in a secularised, humanistic religion, replacing the image of Christ. Clearly a considerable distance separates such an appropriation from the character in a Jacobean historical drama. Hamlet may have been recognised in Shakespeare's time as a Christian hero: but Shakespeare could hardly have foreseen a cultural situation in which his character would be canonised as the saint of a new religious philosophy.

(ii) The odd paradox by which the representation of a living form is encrusted with decay while the dead object is smooth and unblemished, arises from a simple fact: that generations of tourists have travelled to Stratford, stood before that statue and touched the skull. Unconsciously, unintentionally, the innocent visitor finds him/herself participating in a quasi-religious rite, reaching the end of a pilgrimage and laying reverent hands on the symbol of Hamlet's meditative philosophical vision. I did it myself before I realised what I was doing!

DISCUSSION

One scholar has demonstrated that the image of the figure with the skull was by no means an invention of Shakespeare's, but a traditional device often used in portraiture, and exemplified in its most famous representation in a portrait by Franz Hals of a young man holding a skull.[12] The attraction of the emblem seems to have consisted in its juxtaposition of youth, beauty and vigour with the symbolism of death. This *memento mori* tradition was not simply a morbid reminder of mortality, but an incentive to fuller living.

Modern scholarship had to unearth this tradition by comparitive cultural analysis and historical research. When we look at images of Hamlet with the skull, we don't see that tradition embodied in a figurative representation: we see Shakespeare's Hamlet. The tradition has been subsumed into a dominant representation inseparably associated with the name of the great British playwright. In this particular form, the tradition changes its meaning: the skull becomes a kind of visual aid by means of which the philosopher-prince instructs us in the great mysteries of life and death: 'To be or not to be, that is the question' (3.1.56); 'The undiscovered country, from whose bourn/ No traveller returns' (3.1.79–80); 'There is a special providence in the fall of a sparrow' (5.2.192).

There is a further extension to this use of the figure of Hamlet as quasi-religious symbolism. Read the following lines from a poem, an elegaic address to Shakespeare, by Delmore Schwarz. How does the poem link the figure of Hamlet to the character of his creator?

> Gold morning, sweet prince, black night has always
> descended and has always ended,
> Gold morning, prince of Avon, Sovereign and King
> Of reality, hope and speech, may all the angels sing
> With all the sweetness and all the truth with which you
> sang of anything and everything.[13]

The phrase 'sweet prince' is of course used of Hamlet by Horatio (5.2.338). Here it is applied to Shakespeare himself; 'Prince of Avon' conflates 'prince of Denmark' with 'Swan of Avon'; and the flights of angels that sing Hamlet to his rest are here invoked to celebrate Hamlet's creator. The philosopher-prince who gazes stoically through the mysteries of life and death is identified with the transcendent wisdom of the dramatist.

DISCUSSION

Both these examples testify to a particular kind of appropriation or manipulation of the Renaissance play in the service of a quasi-religious ideology. The kinds of meaning attributed to the icon of Hamlet-with-skull may have nothing to do with the original Jacobean play, and can obviously be resisted in modern performances like Buzz Goodbody's: but they are potent meanings, and they belong to a powerful ideological structure in which Shakespeare appears as a transcendent repository of infinite and eternal moral wisdom and human understanding. It is necessary to be aware of such meanings, since if we do not use them they tend to use us. We cannot ignore or deny them, or return to the original object, the play, as if they were not there. But we can hope to understand their relationship with whatever thing the play itself really is.

2.   Stage and Text

I

One way of pursing that elusive object is to regain a sense of what Shakespeare's play *Hamlet* was in its original context of production, before the history of interpretation we have just been sketching began to mediate the play to readers and audiences. It is easy to take for granted the modern edited text of a Shakespeare play as a manifestation of the object as it really is: but such texts are the result of centuries of scholarly research and critical discussion, and in many ways do not even resemble the kind of cultural product that *Hamlet* was in 1600. In such editions the 'play' has been given a kind of absolute finality and fixity of form, held rigid by a constricting framework of critical introduction, explanatory notes, appendices and so forth, which in the Renaissance theatre it could never have had. The texts of the play we now accept as 'Shakespeare's *Hamlet*' originated with the scholarly editors of the eighteenth century: already for them the plays were pieces of a remote history which had to be interpreted, explained, and reconstructed for the benefit of modern readers. Valuable and necessary as that process may be, it produces the play in forms which are significantly different from those it inhabited in the historical moment of its original production.

We will look first of all at some facts about the theatre for which Shakespeare wrote his plays, and then examine the physical space of that theatre itself as the originating context of *Hamlet*. We are so accustomed to knowing these plays as *books* that it requires some imaginative effort to realise that they were very much pieces of *theatre* before they became works of literature. Shakespeare and the other dramatists of the time wrote for the stage, not for publication: the plays they wrote were not initially regarded, in law or by social convention, as the personal property of the author, but the property of the acting company which commissioned or bought them from him. There was no law of copyright as there is now: there was a state register of publications in which you could enter a title 'to be staied', thus establishing a claim to it, but this was in practice no protection against piracy. A *Hamlet* play (presumably Shakespeare's) 'as acted by the Lord Chamberlain's Men' was registered in 1602: but that did not stop the 'unauthorised' First Quarto from appearing in 1603 (see below, pp. 30–34). At any one time in London several prestigious acting companies would be competing for audiences, and eager to secure new writing to attract an audience. Playwrights could be under contract to an acting company to deliver so many plays a year: and they might be involved in the affairs of the company in other ways. Shakespeare for example was an actor, a 'sharer' (part owner) and resident writer in the company initially known as the Lord Chamberlain's Men, and subsequently on the accession of James I as the King's Men or His Majesty's Servants. The actual process by which the plays were written and performed did not involve publication at all: the writer's manuscript was copied by a scribe; that transcript was submitted to the Master ·of the Revels, the officer of state responsible for approving and censoring plays; and then used as a basis for a 'prompt-book'. Additional separate copies were made of each actor's lines, with cues. Even the actors, therefore, did not possess what we think of as 'the whole play' in a printed or written form. The acting companies were extremely reluctant to see their plays pass into print at all.

Consider the format of the title-page from the earliest printed text of Hamlet:

The
Tragicall Historie of
HAMLET
Prince of Denmark

By William Shakespeare

As it hath been diverse times acted by his Highnesse servants in
the Cittie of London: as also in the two Universities of Cambridge
and Oxford, and elsewhere

At London printed for N. L. and John Trundell
1603

(i) What is significant about its attribution in the light of the preceding discussion?
(ii) On the basis of the facts given above, ask yourself why the acting companies were averse to their plays passing into print.

(i) The play is attributed to its author: but the title-page also advertises it in terms of the acting company which performed it and to whom it belonged. Early plays by Shakespeare were published without the name of the author (a common practice) but with the acting company's name in its place.

(ii) As there were no copyright laws as we would recognise them in Elizabethan England, once a play was in print there was nothing to stop a rival acting company putting it on for themselves.

DISCUSSION

The whole purpose of publication is to render something communicable to larger numbers of people via the trade in printed matter. Authors, publishers and booksellers naturally wish to retain their monopoly over that circulation, so copyright laws exist to forbid unauthorised duplication. To the entrepreneur who ran a theatre, or to the collective of sharers who constituted the acting company, the play was commercially viable only as performance: the big money was in theatre audiences, not in expensive printed books. Once the play had exhausted its popularity in the theatre, the company would sell the text to a publisher to salvage a few pounds: or a company could be pushed into printing a play by the appearance of an unauthorised 'pirate' edition. The Elizabethan acting companies can be compared with the major film companies of today who seek to prevent the copying and distribution of their productions on video-tape.

We will consider the various types of printed form in which the plays did appear towards the end of this chapter (see below, pp. 30–34). But what important consequences did these conditions of production have for the original nature of a Shakespeare play? The 'text' of a play must have existed within an acting company primarily as a script, a 'text-for-performance': a basic structure or score on which a theatrical presentation could be improvised and executed. The dramatic event itself could not have been controlled or corrected by the existence of some 'authentic' text: so the play must in those conditions have been much more *alterable* than we often imagine. Far from being a fixed embodiment of Shakespeare's artistry, the play must have been a changing, developing, malleable entity, constantly shifting in shape and form as the actors experimented, improvised, tested out the play in rehearsal and before their audiences.

If in performance the play was not directed by a fixed textual structure, then the performance was in an absolute sense the making of the play: a process influenced by many contingent factors, including the play-text, the presence or absence of the writer as an active participant, the character of the players themselves, the physical conditions of the playhouse, the tangible presence of a vociferously participating audience.[1]

As we shall see shortly, the evidence for this lies in the Elizabethan play-texts themselves. The important conclusion to draw here is that Shakespeare's theatre was not directly or consciously concerned with the production of literary masterpieces, but rather with staging exciting, entertaining and thought-provoking plays, which were thought of primarily as a form of cultural interaction between players and audiences in a theatre. The now revered canon of Shakespeare's writings was in a sense a side-effect of his main professional business. It is true that in the course of the period in question there was emerging a different concept of authorship, in which the writing is seen as the product of a creative individual: and playwrights like Ben Jonson, who claimed for theatrical writing the higher title of 'poetry', were prominent advocates of this new 'writerly' status. It was in line with this attitude that two of Shakespeare's acting colleagues collected his plays together and published them in the text now known as the 'First Folio' in 1623. That was, however, ten years after Shakespeare's death: there is no evidence at all that he himself was in any way concerned to constitute his plays into this modern form, the totality of the writer's *oeuvre*.

II

Let us now consider the physical conditions of the theatre in which *Hamlet* was first performed around 1600. Study illustration 6. This is a drawing of the interior of the Swan theatre, probably the most valuable single piece of evidence we have about the early Renaissance theatres.[2] The Globe theatre on Bankside, built in 1599, where *Hamlet* was first performed, would have been in all essentials similar to the Swan. I will first of all give you some guidance as to how this drawing may be interpreted, and then ask you to consider some questions about it.

The theatres which began to appear on the outskirts of the City of London from 1576 were open air amphitheatres modelled on existing places of entertainment such as bear-baiting arenas. Within a round or polygonal structure, the stage, a large but simple raised platform, occupied a central position. At the rear of the stage stood a flat wall, behind which was the 'tiring-house' (where the actors 'attired') surmounted by a gallery. Thus the rear of the stage was known as the 'tiring-house facade': in the drawing it is marked as

6 *The Swan theatre*

'mimorum aedes', the 'actors' house'. Two doors provided the means of entrance and exit between tiring-house and stage. A roof supported on two columns covered half the stage, and above that you can see the 'hut' which would contain any machinery needed for lowering actors or props down onto the stage from above. The audience space consisted of a yard in which people had to stand, surrounding the stage on three sides; and galleries (in the drawing 'orchestia') where seating accomodation was available at a higher price. The gallery above the stage may have been used for musicians or for additional spectators: it was also required as an acting area 'above' at some points in some plays: but that does not necessarily exclude its occupation by either spectators or musicians.[3] The physical resources available to the players were thus basically very simple: a bare, flat stage (containing a trapdoor for ghosts, devils etc. to enter), two doors for entrances and exits, and a playing area 'aloft'.

So the kind of theatre in which *Hamlet* came into being was very different from a typical modern theatre. There are of course many types of theatre in existence today – studio theatres, 'theatres-in-the-round', and so forth – but by 'typical' I mean the sort of theatre, based on Victorian models, to be found in London's West End, in most of the major provincial theatres, at the National Theatre or the Royal Shakespeare Theatre at Stratford-upon-Avon. If your experience of theatre-going is not very wide, think of a cinema: a flat wall with a (curtained) rectangular screen and the audience grouped in seats opposite to it; the screen is brightly illuminated, the auditorium in darkness. The shape of a cinema is based on the Victorian theatre or music-hall, with its rectangular picture-frame stage and proscenium arch, its stage lighting and darkened auditorium, and most of the audience (apart from the stage-boxes) sitting end on to face the stage. Similar stages are often to be found in school halls, hospitals and other municipal buildings. Some theatres (such as the Royal Shakespeare Theatre at Stratford-upon-Avon) have the proscenium arch removed to create an 'open' stage: but the basic shape remains – the spectator looks through a rectangular frame at an illuminated spectacle.

Compare these two different theatrical models, using the Swan drawing and the two drawings in illustration 7. What do you think are likely to be the chief differences between performances in an Elizabethan and a modern theatre?

These are some of the things that might have occurred to you:
(i) the Elizabethan theatres were open air buildings, whereas now we think of theatre as an interior event;

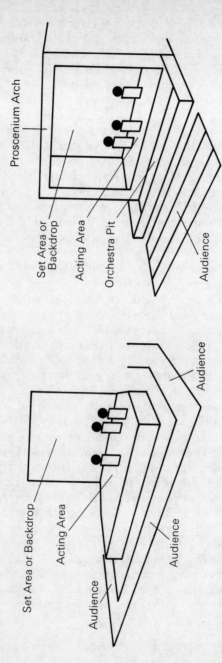

7 *Renaissance and Modern theatres*

(ii) the only lighting available to such a theatre was therefore natural daylight – so there could be no special effects of lighting, and the members of the audience could all see one another;

(iii) many members of the audience would be standing for the performance, in very close proximity to the stage – something we would expect as spectators at a football match, but not at a play;

(iv) there was no pictorial scenery and there were no stage sets to localise the action in a particular place (compare with illustration 5, from an eighteenth century edition of *Hamlet* where the setting is clearly an interior one);

(v) the audience would be surrounding the stage on three, possibly four sides in the manner of a 'theatre-in-the-round' – so the actors had to play in three dimensions, and the separation between stage and audience which we regard as normal did not exist in the same degree;

(vi) the only equivalent to a modern 'set' is the bench on which the actors depicted are sitting. This must either have remained on stage throughout, thus being used as whatever piece of furniture – a chair, a throne, a bed – the action demanded; or it must have been carried on and off in full view of the audience.

Let us consider the action of *Hamlet* in terms of the theatrical resources – setting, lighting, major props – we would need to stage it. The action is identified as taking place in various locations within the castle of Elsinore and elsewhere. Scenes take place on the battlements, in a great hall, in other rooms, in the Queen's bedroom. Act 5, scene one takes place in a cemetery, and there is one scene (4.2) in an unidentified exterior location. No special effects of lighting are needed except the distinction between day and night. A throne, a bed and a grave are needed. Characters have to be concealed – Claudius and Polonius hide behind an arras (3.4) and Polonius hides in the same place for the last time in Act 3, scene four. We would need the means to stage a 'play-within-a-play'; the ghost would presumably require some kind of 'special effects'; and Ophelia's grave would have to be suitable for two men to fight in.

Now look again at the Swan drawing. How many of these theatrical needs, as we would understand them today, would that stage be able to satisfy?

Not many of them! Without movable scenery, the stage could not depict different locations: it remains the same space and retains the same visual appearance throughout the entire play.

DISCUSSION

There simply were no effects of lighting: the theatre had no means of distinguishing light from darkness (compare again with illustration 5: the shadows indicate a studied use of artificial light). Major props would have to be minimal: one bench could perhaps have served as Claudius' throne, Gertrude's bed, and a beir on which to carry Ophelia's body. Though scholars tend to think that as the throne (or 'state' as it was sometimes known) was a necessary prop for so many plays that it might have been a substantial or permanent feature of the stage.

Concealment presents a special problem. Where, on that bare stage, could an actor hide? Later theatres introduced a curtained and recessed 'inner stage' between the two doors, which would obviously have provided a 'discovery space' suitable for such concealments and revelations. But there certainly was no such inner stage at the Swan, and there seems to me no strong reason for supposing that there was one at the Globe. Any machinery of concealment must then have been pretty notional – a movable screen for example – or 'hiding' could have been a purely *conventional* gesture, with Polonius remaining in full view of the audience and Hamlet simply pretending not to see him. If that seems to you unlikely, look at the 'graveyard scene' (5.1.185–221). Hamlet and Horatio there 'withdraw' to somewhere where the rest of the cast can't see them: yet they must actually remain in full view and hearing of both cast and audience.

A trapdoor in the centre of the stage was the means by which apparitions from another world could enter the acting area. The ghost in *Hamlet* is not averse to more conventional methods of entry and exit, since he enters 'with Hamlet' (at 1.4.87.), and leaves his wife's chamber by walking 'out at the portal' (3.4.137). On the other hand, the ghost certainly spent some time under the platform stage, since he cries out from there (1.5.150) and Hamlet jokes about 'this fellow in the cellerage'. Although some 'special effects' were employed to suggest the ghost's supernatural status, he was basically played by a costumed actor walking around the stage in broad daylight.

It is generally assumed that the trapdoor in the centre of the stage also served as Ophelia's grave: the stage directions stipulate clearly that Laertes and Hamlet 'leap into the grave', suggesting that the actors jumped down a level. This seems to me unlikely: the trapdoor was used to admit one actor at a time, and it seems improbable that it would have been larger than necessary for that purpose. On this kind of stage, the simple act of laying Ophelia down on the platform would make that space, in the audience's eyes, into a 'grave'; Hamlet and Laertes could simply fight around the body.

It goes without saying that the stage of the Renaissance public playhouse, at its most primitive and unfurnished as represented in the Swan drawing, must have been capable of providing the theatrical resources necessary for producing *Hamlet*: but only on condition that a certain approach to the drama was adopted. The theatre must have been largely or completely non-illusionistic: no attempt being considered necessary to make the stage look like a real place. Darkness could never be made visible as in a modern theatre, so a night scene would have to be defined by the dialogue (as in the opening scene, or after *The Murder of Gonzago* when Hamlet declares ''Tis now the very witching time of night' (3.2.349); or indicated by the actors wearing night-dress – in the 1603 text of *Hamlet* the ghost logically enters his wife's bedroom in 3.4 'in his night gowne'.[4] 'Concealment' was probably as nominal as it is in pantomime, with the 'hidden' actors in full view of the audience. If the theatre did not have a recessed inner stage, Hamlet's play, performed with the Danish court constituted as audience, could have been staged only by arranging groupings of actors on the flat stage. Ophelia's burial and the fight in the grave could well have been 'mimed' rather than represented.

A further point to be aware of is that the acting companies of this period did not perform only in the purpose-built theatres. There were still strong traditions of commissioned private entertainment whereby the actors would be paid to perform at court, in a hall of the nobility or at a citizen's house. The actors of Shakespeare's company might have played at the Globe in the afternoon and repeated the performance in another place, where they would not be able to rely on the availability of theatrical devices, in the evening. In addition the companies continued to 'tour the provinces' after they were established in their own purpose-built theatres, thus taking their productions to many different venues and locations. They would not always have had a trapdoor in which to bury Ophelia.

Some scholars and critics would argue that the Elizabethan actors aimed at achieving a much more naturalistic dramatic medium than the one I am proposing. On pp. 51 and 57 of the recommended edition you will find drawings by C. Walter Hodges suggesting the use of a recessed and curtained inner stage, and of the trapdoor as a grave: suggesting, in short, that every opportunity was taken to make the stage representational and illusionistic. Another view can be found in Robert Weimann's *Shakespeare and the Popular Tradition in the Theatre*.[5] He argues, by analogy with popular theatrical forms like mystery plays, that the upstage area would be used to convey a sense of realism and historical veracity; while when the actors came downstage and entered into direct relationship with the audience, the illusion would be suspended or broken. You might feel that Weimann's view proposes a more flexible theatrical space, capable both of realism and non-representational performance, than the anti-illusionist theatre for which I have argued.

Hamlet is particularly noted for its use of the device of soliloquy: an emphasis which has been understood to indicate a new kind of interest in the individual and a new depth of psychological insight. In Laurence Olivier's film version, the soliloquies were done in voice-over: they ceased to be a theatrical language and became the dialect of the character's mind. How were such speeches done in the early theatres?

Imagine an actor performing a soliloquy on the stage of what I described above as a 'typical modern theatre'. Then imagine the same speech done at the Globe: a bare platform stage, an audience crowded round, everything visible in conditions of daylight performance. Use illustration 7 to help you visualise this contrast.

In the first example the actor under modern stage lighting can't really see the audience, so conditions make it impossible for him to address them directly. Such stage conditions force the soliloquy back onto the individual character, so we observe him engaged in an act of self-communion: we overhear him talking or thinking to himself. We see him brightly lit, isolated, suspended in time in the frame of a picture.

On the Globe stage it would be much more difficult, perhaps impossible, to ignore the audience: and much more natural to speak to them.

DISCUSSION

That condition changes the whole nature of the act of communication. A question becomes no longer a confession of personal dubeity, but a proposition for debate: 'To be or not to be?: that is the question', addressed to the audience for their consideration, becomes more actual as a problem, and perhaps more involving as a theatrical experience, than the objective representation of a melancholy hero contemplating suicide. Perhaps the spectators depicted by Dickens (see p. 2 above) were responding to the play more in the manner of the original audiences than the relatively passive, quiescent audiences of today. An actor would do well in such a popular theatre to forestall heckling by involving the audience from the outset!

We will be returning to this argument when we consider Act 3, where Hamlet's advice to the players (3.2) presents special problems, since it has generally been accepted as Shakespeare's own personal observations on dramatic theory, and evidence that he held a creed of theatrical naturalism. I will leave this topic for the moment by indicating some of the conclusions that have been drawn from these facts. The various works cited in the Notes and Further Reading will indicate where you might go to follow up the various arguments.

(i) It has been argued that the Elizabethan theatres obliged their audiences to concentrate above all else on the *actors*. Having little to offer in the way of visual spectacle or special theatrical effects, the theatres relied on the power and vigour of the players themselves:

> ... a close, almost exclusive attention to the actors sustained enjoyment and discovery. The originality did not spring from some new mode of staging or some new dominant theme, but was the result of an exploration of Shakespeare's plays by actors who lived with his roles and modified their performances from night to night, and acted with giant imagination and resource for a free audience.[6]

(ii) Other writers have suggested that such theatres forced a concentration on the *language* of the plays, requiring an attentiveness comparable to that of literary 'textual criticism'. The fact that today we find Shakespeare's language intrinsically, and not just historically, difficult induces many people to doubt whether his original audiences – some of whom would have been illiterate – could have understood all or much of the plays. But it is important to remember that in a still partially oral culture speech has to be capable of embodying all the complexity and sophistication we put into writing. Television is a good example of an oral and visual medium with a highly complex language, which we know so well we forget that it has to be learned: but it can be understood by an illiterate person. It is possible that an unlettered Elizabethan playgoer might have been able to apprehend the subtleties and complexities of the verse more easily than we can.[7]

(iii) Another view is that the physical emptiness of the theatre demanded an extraordinary degree of imaginative participation on the part of the spectators, who were urged (for example by the Chorus in *Henry V*) to visualise realistic settings for themselves. The bare stage was therefore a positive advantage, since it required an active effort of the spectator's imagination, rather than the more passive quiescence in elaborate stage spectacle we nowadays take for granted.[8]

(iv) A different view can be found in the comments of Bertolt Brecht, who saw Shakespeare's theatre not as a theatre of illusion, but as one of 'alienation' – in which the audience would be encouraged *not* to believe in the reality of what was being presented; but rather to retain an awareness of its constructed, theatrical nature. '*A Midsummer Night's Dream* was played in daylight and it was daylight when the ghost in Hamlet appeared. What price illusion?'[9] Again for Brecht the absence of 'location' was a positive feature of the Renaissance theatre: since it enabled the drama to maintain a variable distance between representation and reality.

III

Compare these two passages:
 (i) To be, or not to be, that is the Question:
    Whether 'tis nobler in the mind to suffer
    The Slings and Arrowes of outragious Fortune,
    Or to takes Armes against a sea of troubles,
    And by opposing end them: to dye, to sleepe
    No more …
(ii) To be, or not to be, I there's the point,
    To Die, to sleep, is that all: I all:
    No, to sleepe, to dreame, I mary there it goes …

As the first passage is probably the most famous speech in Shakespeare it will be easily recognisable: it is quoted here from the first collected edition of Shakespeare's plays, the 'First Folio' of 1623. The second is a version of the same speech as recorded in the first text of *Hamlet* to be printed, the 'First Quarto' of 1603.[10] Not only is the language different: in each text the speech is positioned differently too. In the Quarto it comes before the players arrive at Elsinore: in the Folio it occurs between the first scene with the players and the play they perform.

Write some notes on what seem to you the obvious differences between the two, and on what you can conjecture to have been their respective functions in the action.

Example (ii) is simpler and more concise: it contains only one idea, that of suicide, and there is no reference to the alternative possibility of taking up arms against fortune. The arrival of the players in this version jolts Hamlet out of his suicidal propensities, and provides him not only with the opportunity but with the very idea of performing some kind of action. In the 1623 version the speech itself contains a debate between two alternatives, and the play-within-a-play can be seen as Hamlet's application of the possibility of 'taking up arms'. In the Quarto version the meanings are all contained in the events of the action: in the Folio the meanings are more psychological, as the debate is internalised in the character's mind.

DISCUSSION

The First Quarto of 1603 claims on the title-page that this is the 'Tragicall Historie of / HAMLET / *Prince of Denmark* / By William Shakespeare / As it hath been diverse times acted by his Highnesse servants in the Cittie of London: as also in the two Universities of Cambridge and Oxford, and elsewhere'. The Second Quarto (some copies of which are dated 1604, some 1605) bears a different title: 'The Tragicall Historie of HAMLET, Prince of Denmarke, by William Shakespeare / Newly imprinted and enlarged to almost as much againe as it was, according to the true and perfect Coppie'. The latter text is substantially the same as that of the Folio text of 1623, though it is longer, and passages appear in each which are not in the other. The First Quarto is what is generally known as a 'bad Quarto': 'a corrupt, unauthorised version of an abridged version of Shakespeare's play'.[11] The Second Quarto, in claiming to be based on 'the true and perfect Coppie', appears to be a more authentic form of the play.

It is conjectured that the First Quarto was pirated – perhaps recorded and reconstructed from memory, possibly by one of the actors who performed in it – and published without permission of the author or his company. The Second Quarto would then have been a publication by author and company of the true text. If that were the case, there would be no doubt that the Second Quarto represents both Shakespeare's intended text and the version the company used for performances.

But this received account brings in its wake a host of problems. We do not know how the 1603 and 1604/5 texts found their way into print; but we do know that the same publisher, Nicholas Ling, printed both texts. We do not know what the Second Quarto claims to be a true and perfect copy of – the author's manuscript? The transcript prepared and submitted to the censor? The prompt-book? What we do know is that neither the Second Quarto nor the Folio texts could have represented an acting version: they are both far too long. It would take at least four hours to play the Second Quarto, even at high speed. In the nineteenth century perform-ances of the play were mounted using all the extant material from the two longer texts: known as 'the Entirity', this took six hours to play. Jacobean open-air performances took place approximately between 2 and 4 p.m., the hours of optimum daylight; and the Chorus in *Romeo and Juliet* speaks of 'the two-hours traffic of our stage'.

It is obvious from the fact alone that the First Quarto represents an acting version of the play. Whether it was a first, hastily prepared script, or a cut down touring version; whether it was taken down from an actual performance, or hurriedly assembled from an uncompleted author's draft, we will never know: what we do know is that it comes closer than the other texts to actual Jacobean stage practice. The text of the play with which we are familiar may well have been copied from the author's manuscript: but it is not the version of the play seen by Jacobean audiences. The received text is certainly readable, but it is not *performable* within the time-scale available to theatre audiences: it is almost always cut in performance. We have to ask therefore why the more *written* forms of the play, which can be conceived as products of the study, should have been given such priority over the *acted* version to be found in the First Quarto. Was Shakespeare the kind of writer who attached great importance and value, as subsequent ages have done, to the specific shape of the products of his pen, and who might well have regarded the theatre as a degrading influence on it? Or – given that Shakespeare was not only a playwright but also a theatrical professional, an actor and member of a theatrical co-operative business, and a shareholder in the Globe Theatre – is it perhaps more likely that he was involved to a greater extent in the productions of the theatre than in the products of the study?

Compare these versions of Hamlet's dying speech. What seem to you the chief differences between them?

  (i) O fie *Horatio*, and if thou shouldst die,
      What a scandale wouldst thou leave behind?
      What tongue should tell the story of our deaths,
      If not from thee? O my heart sinckes *Horatio*,
      Mine eyes have lost their sight, my tongue his vse:
      Farewel *Horatio*, heauen receiue my soule.

                                                                        (1603)

(ii) O god *Horatio*, what a wounded name
     Things standing thus vnknowne, shall I leaue behind me?
     If thou did'st euer hold me in thy hart,
     Absent thee from felicity a while,
     And in this harsh world drawe they breath in paine
     To tell my story: ... O I die *Horatio*,
     The potent poyson quite ore-crows my spirit,
     I cannot liue to heare the newes from *England*.
     But I doe prophecie th'ellection lights
     On *Fortinbrasse*, he has my dying voyce,
     So tell him, with all th'occurrants more and lesse
     Which have solicited, the rest is silence.

                                                              (1605)[12]

Again, 1603 gives a condensed version of the speech, with no reference to Fortinbras, and no poetic eloquence: 'the rest is silence' and 'Absent thee from felicity a while' do not appear in the First Quarto. The nomination of Fortinbras as successor enhances the impression of Hamlet as a noble, responsible and self-sacrificial character.

DISCUSSION

The gestures of eloquence, conferring a lyrical elegaic quality much loved by Victorian audiences (performances would often end with 'the rest is silence') are the details most prized by literary criticism of the play, which naturally favours the 'readable' rather than the 'actable' text. When Matthew Arnold provided a series of examples of little gems of English poetry, self-evidently containing the qualities of poetic value and of high seriousness, he quoted the 'Absent thee from felicity' lines.[13] The longer version of the speech was however certainly played in Shakespeare's time: it appears in the Folio with the addition of an interesting performance detail:

     The rest is silence. O, o, o, o. *Dyes*[14]

I know of no modern text to have reproduced those terminal 'o's, the stage signs of a death-agony. Editors may well prefer the musical dying fall of 'the rest is silence': but in doing so they evince a singular lack of respect for what actually happened on the Jacobean stage when *Hamlet* was performed.

The textual scholarship of Shakespeare's plays is a complex and meticulously detailed science: if you want to know more about it, Further Reading will guide you. I have drawn these matters to your attention at this point in order to demonstrate that in its original form a play like *Hamlet* could never have had the kind of fixity of structure and form suggested by a modern edition: it was a fluid, constantly changing, iterable phenomenon. Philip Edwards makes the point well:

> In searching for a solution to the play's textual problems, we should not imagine that we are ever likely to find ourselves with a single definitive text. The study of the early texts of *Hamlet* is the study of a play in motion. Earlier editors of *Hamlet* may have thought that 'a complete and final version' of the play was the object of their search, but nowadays we are more ready to accept what centuries of theatrical history tell us – that what is written for the theatre often undergoes considerable modification as it moves from the writer's desk towards performance on the stage and also during performance. We must be prepared for the possibility that the variations in the text of *Hamlet* are not alternative versions of a single original text but representations of different stages in the play's development.[15]

It will be salutary to remember, as we search the play for meaning and interpretation, that we are not dealing with some form of Holy Writ fixed and consolidated by the great master-poet: but with something that was from the very beginning pluralistic and iterable, alterable and productive of many diverse meanings.

3. Psychology of Revenge

Having said all that, to work on *Hamlet* in any way at all involves working on a text – whether that text be a scholarly edition, a script for production, a prompt-book, a film or TV version, or an actual performance – and we will be working on the kind of modern edition, drawn from the Second Quarto and First Folio texts, which manifest the play in its most 'literary', most *written* form. At the same time, we will be attempting to preserve, by keeping in mind the dimension of performance and the variability of texts, an awareness of the play's true plurality, its openness to interpretation and diversity of meaning.

I

I would like you now to work through some early scenes in Act 1, moving towards a detailed discussion of the crucial fifth scene between Hamlet and the ghost. A consideration of that scene will provoke an extended discussion of revenge, as an aesthetic pattern and a contemporary (Renaissance) ethical problem. Finally I will offer some more concise guidelines on the analysis and interpretation of other scenes involving 'minor' characters (though that definition, like the related distinction between 'main-plot' and 'sub-plot', may not be a particularly useful one to use for *Hamlet* – see below, pp. 53–4).

Give a careful reading to 1.2, paying particular attention to Claudius as well as to Hamlet, and bearing in mind the following questions:
(i) what impression do you receive of Claudius, as king and as man, from his speeches in this scene?
(ii) In this scene Hamlet begins to make comparisons ('Hyperion to a satyr', 1.2.140) between his dead father and his uncle. Do such comparisons occur to the reader before Hamlet broaches them?
(iii) What general view do we receive of the Danish court? And what sense do we get of Hamlet's position within it?
(iv) Consider the phrase 'actions that a man might play' (1.2.84). What exactly does Hamlet mean? And is there anything odd about the expression given the context in which it appears?
(v) What emotions are expressed in Hamlet's first soliloquy (1.219–158)? What appears to be their root cause?

(i) There are two ways of receiving Claudius as he appears at the beginning of the play. We can (a) read our knowledge of what is later disclosed back into our apprehension of his character before that disclosure is made; or (b) we can set aside our ultimate awareness that Claudius is at least a murderer, if not an incestuous usurper into the bargain, and view him more 'objectiveley'.

DISCUSSION

You might feel that this is difficult to do: if we know Claudius killed his brother, how can such a primal crime be ignored? Yet it is a necessary part of the experience and the pleasures of fiction that we agree to suppress or defer certain kinds of knowledge about ultimate happenings in order to become engaged in the process and development of a story. In the course of doing that, as we shall see, alternative readings sometimes become available.

If we measure Claudius from the outset by his crime, he must appear, as he speaks of 'Hamlet our dear brother's death', a flagrant hypocrite, his ostentatious attempt to balance 'sorrow' and 'discretion' an opportunistic expediency: and the elaborate syntactic emphasis given to the royal plural could be a deliberate attempt to affirm sovereignty, perhaps in a context where that sovereignty might well be questioned.

> That we with wisest sorrow think on him
> Together with remembrance of ourselves.   (1.2.6–7)

If on the other hand we agree to suppress our prospective knowledge of the murder, Claudius will appear an exemplar of reason and moderation, advocating the only possible attitude to bereavement: and this whole speech to Hamlet (1.2.87–117) may seem an admirable recommendation of fortitude and stoic courage in the face of inevitable personal loss.

(ii) Comparisons between the present and former kings arise inevitably from the text, since Claudius is confronting a situation almost identical to that faced by old Hamlet (see 1.1.80–95), a military challenge from the disinherited prince of neighbouring Norway.

DISCUSSION

The contrast in methods of dealing with that threat is very plain: old Hamlet was challenged by old Fortinbras to a chivalric duel, and achieved victory in a heroic single combat. Confronted by the invasion of Fortinbras' son, also confusingly named after his father (Scandinavians of that period showing little imagination in the provision of names) Claudius doesn't offer to fight him, but sends a diplomatic embassy to Fortinbras' uncle, 'old Norway', in a (successful) effort to divert the danger by political negotiation. Something odd has happened to Denmark in the course of a move from one king to another; it is almost as if the state has lived through a great historical transition from the heroic tribal past of Saxo's saga to a Renaissance court much closer to Shakespeare's own historical moment.

(Notice the way in which the play draws attention to the *symmetry* of these royal families of Denmark and Norway: in each case a king has been killed, a brother succeeds, and a son is left under the obligation of revenge. The inevitable comparison between Hamlet and Fortinbras is explored in detail in 4.4.)

Once again, the contrast between old Hamlet and Claudius can be viewed in two ways. Old Hamlet can be juxtaposed to his brother in the terms proposed by Hamlet himself: a chivalric and heroic warrior compared to a crafty and unscrupulous politician. But if we accepted that comparison we would be assuming two things: that Hamlet's own version of events is the one we should accept; and that the play can automatically assume in its readers or spectators a preference for the simplicity of heroic values over the devious complexities of more modern political methods. But can that be assumed? Given the choice, under which king would most people rather live: the one who is prepared to gamble a section of his kingdom on the result of a passage of arms; or the one who preserves the stability of his state by peaceful and reasonable methods of persuasion and negotiation? Which alternative is it likely Shakespeare's contemporaries would have preferred?

(iii) Claudius is obviously working very hard to hold his court together in unanimity of feeling and opinion: and apart from Hamlet no member of that court seems inclined to resist or question his power or his style of government. On the other hand that unanimity may be a spurious and superficial integration of a political body which is actually much more divided and fragmented than Claudius' rhetoric admits.

DISCUSSION

Both Hamlet and Laertes wish to leave Denmark – Laertes to France, Hamlet to university in Wittenberg. Claudius permits Laertes to leave, but seeks – partly by using Gertrude's influence – to persuade Hamlet to remain. The difference in treatment is not explained, and we may entertain a suspicion that Claudius wants Hamlet close at hand for purposes as yet undisclosed. On the other hand we may assume that Claudius remains unsatisfied in his attempt to reintegrate Hamlet back into the social order the prince appears, from his contemptuous asides and his resistance to proferred persuasion and counsel, to be rejecting. One telling detail provides a hint as to Claudius' methods of government: where he dispatches Voltemand and Cornelius to Norway

> Giving you no further personal power
> To business with the king, more than the scope
> Of these dilated articles allows. (1.2.36–9)

A cautious vigilance seeks here to constrain any independence of judgement or action his subjects might manifest: is this a state in which the apparently genial sovereign exercises a subtle despotic control? (see below, pp. 87–9) or one in which the need to affirm and establish 'order' can be permitted to over-ride individual rights and liberties?

Superficially at least the court accepts the uniformity of style and behaviour imposed by Claudius. It is that sense of social cohesion, or perhaps conformity, that makes Hamlet stand out with particular sharpness as a uniquely alienated individual. The internal stage directions, with their reference to the prince's 'customary suits of solemn black' single him out – since presumably everyone else has forsaken their mourning after Claudius' injunction to be cheerful. Hamlet even rejects the formal modes of address which invoke both his actual relationships with other people and his social and familial identity: when the king calls him 'cousin' and 'son', he denies both claims – 'a little more than kin, and less than kind'. Claudius' intimacy with both the dead father and the living mother make his proximity of relationship uncomfortably close; yet Hamlet feels that he is not of the same 'kind' (family or species) as the king. He stands apart and refuses social integration: singular, elusive, not to be assigned. Against the advocacy of both Gertrude and Claudius, who counsel the same recognition of the 'common' lot of mortality, Hamlet asserts a uniqueness of feeling and a deep conviction of difference – the observable forms of mourning are 'actions that a man might play' (1.2.84) while he lays claim to an authentic singularity of experience and feeling – 'I have that within which passes show' (1.2.85). In the course of insisting that his eccentricities of behaviour are rooted in the depth of his grief, Hamlet expresses a strong refusal to be limited and constrained by the ordinary social definitions of the world.

(iv) The outward signs of grief can be *acted*, simulated, assumed or affected, without any corresponding reality of feeling. There is nothing odd about the expression if we are reading the play as a kind of novel: but we have to remember that the context is a dramatic one, the world of a play.

DISCUSSION

The distinction assumed, between appearance and reality, 'acting' (in the theatrical sense) and 'action' (in the sense of performing a deed) is fundamental to the novel as a form – partly because of the effectiveness of its narrative strategies in locating contradictions between observable behaviour and inner experience. But here the identification of acting with fraudulent deception, and the claim to a higher authenticity of inner truth, are made (paradoxically) by an actor who is himself 'playing' actions, not *doing* them. We may prefer, whether in the theatre or the study, to forget that Hamlet is a simulated character: but a drama which often draws our attention to its own theatricality is likely to make us more aware of the ambiguities which inevitably arise when an actor claims to be, not an actor impersonating feelings and convictions, but a real character expressing authentic experience. The very language we use to describe these relationships has its qualities of ambivalance: words like 'act' and 'perform' can offer tantalisingly to bridge the gap between stage and world, 'play' and 'reality'. As we shall see in discussing the scenes with the players, these self-reflexive allusions to theatre are a basic component of the play's dramatic structure: and Hamlet himself frequently draws on theatrical metaphors to express his anxieties and conflicts, as he 'acts' the part of an 'actor' directed to 'perform' an 'act' of revenge (see below, pp. 67–70).

(v) Hamlet's resistance to imposed definition is expressed in metaphorical form in his first soliloquy:

> O that this too too solid flesh would melt,
> Thaw and resolve itself into a dew ... (1.2.129–30)

Though he has claimed possession of a substantial core of authenticity, here Hamlet's desire is that the body itself should dissolve and lapse ('melt', 'thaw', 'resolve') into elusive and indefinable liquidity. This paradoxical desire of the living being to disintegrate into its constituent elements is a form of death-wish:

> Or that the Everlasting had not fixed
> His canon 'gainst self-slaughter. (1.2.131–2)

The underlying motive for this suicidal despair is an overwhelming disgust with life:

> How weary, stale, flat and unprofitable
> Seem to me all the uses of this world! (1.2.133–4)

The causes of the world-weariness are in turn the death of his father, Claudius' 'o'erhasty marriage' to his mother, and a general sense of decline, decadence and degeneration in the world around him.

DISCUSSION

How are we to understand these powerful feelings, confided to us with great intimacy and immediacy by the device of soliloquy? Let me suggest two somewhat different ways: we can take Hamlet's emotions as having objective as well as subjective validity: that is, they are not only the feelings of a singular character, but accurate descriptions of the nature of the world; or we can view Hamlet in a more self-contained and isolated way, as the possessor of a curiously attractive but also despicably morbid and idealising view of the world, which may or may not correspond to the facts of the case. It seems to me important to be aware of the possibility that readers and audiences can respond *critically* as well as *sympathetically* to Hamlet's professions and propositions. We may accept Hamlet's vision of his dead father as authentic, and judge Claudius, as he does, accordingly. On the contrary we may feel that Hamlet is idealising the memory of his father, and producing from an intense personal grief a generalised vision of the world in decline. Mythological comparisons like 'Hyperion to a satyr' and 'I to Hercules' have the effect of locating the sordid present ('an unweeded garden') in juxtaposition to an idealised version of the past. In myth the individual and the world become one: the death of a hero can signify the extinction of an age. But should we not be cautious how we accept an individual's indictment of a world on the basis of an understandable reverence for the memory of a dead father?

II

The idealisation of the father co-exists with a potent moralising contempt for the mother, whose 'wicked' and 'incestuous' actions render her one of those 'things rank and gross in nature' which possess the world. Once again Hamlet's expansive vision projects the individual fault to a dimension of universal culpability: 'frailty, thy name is woman'. This condemnation of the mother/woman figure clearly has wide and important implications beyond an assessment of Hamlet's 'character': if Gertrude is 'wicked' and 'incestuous', perhaps she deserves the cruel punishment meted out to her at the end of the play. We will consider this again in Chapter Five (see below, pp. 98–99). I am concerned at the moment with the psychological condition revealed by this speech, in particular its strange polarities of idealisation and moral contempt, reverence and disgust, nostalgia and pessimistic despair: and with the problem of whether such a world-view should be accepted as an objective evaluation of Hamlet's Denmark, or apprehended as the singular perspective of a disturbed mind.

Let us consider one crucially important point, which we have not so far mentioned: the fact that Hamlet's contempt for the world and suicidal depression *precede* his encounter with the ghost: his state of mind here is in all essentials identical to that revealed later in the 'To be or not to be' soliloquy, and yet at this point Hamlet has no knowledge (though abundant suspicion) of the fact of his father's murder. The withering scorn of his discourse is thus pointed entirely at his uncle's character, and at his mother's behaviour in rapidly marrying her brother-in-law. The emotional and moral power of Hamlet's language has its own kind of persuasiveness: but many readers and critics have felt that in some sense these emotions of disgust, revulsion and moral contempt are actually stronger than their ostensible causes. T. S. Eliot, in an essay that became famous for its introduction into critical vocabulary of the term 'objective correlative', developed the theory through observations on *Hamlet*.

> The only way of expressing emotion in the form of art is by finding an 'objective correlative'; in other words, a set of objects, a situation, a chain of events which shall be the formula of that *particular* emotion; such that when the external facts, which must terminate in sensory experience, are given, the emotion is immediately evoked ... The artistic 'inevitability' lies in this complete adequacy of the external to the emotion; and this is precisely what is deficient in *Hamlet*. Hamlet (the man) is dominated by an emotion which is inexpressible, because it is in *excess* of the facts as they appear ... Hamlet is up against the difficulty that his disgust is occasioned by his mother, but that his mother is not an adequate equivalent for it; his disgust envelops and exceeds her. It is thus a feeling which he cannot understand; he cannot objectify it, and it therefore remains to poison life and obstruct action.[2]

Eliot's explanation of this disequilibrium between emotion and cause presupposes that the play is a 'failure' as a work of art, because Shakespeare has not succeeded in embodying an objective equivalent of Hamlet's disgust in a plausible action, set of characters or body of images. Gertrude seems innocent and innocuous by comparison with the moral diatribe in which Hamlet frames her.

Eliot's critique of the play was clearly a bold and polemical intervention into a tradition that held *Hamlet* to be a superlative work of art; and we would not now regard such absolute and incontrovertible decisions about what constitutes a 'success' and what a 'failure' in a work of art as particularly useful. Moreover we would be more concerned to identify precisely this anti-feminine disgust, and perhaps less surprised that the object of it should be in some senses an innocent victim. I would grant however that Eliot was responding to real and problematical aspects of the play: in particular its proportion of emotion to action; or (to use a more contemporary critical language) the preponderance of signifying over signification – the interior world of Hamlet's discourse being in some ways a wider and more complex world than the represented social world of Denmark or the dramatic world of the play itself.

Eliot's approach, in its probing curiosity about deeper emotional causes underlying, perhaps even obscured by, the observable facts of a character or situation, clearly has analogies with the psychoanalytic approaches which have chosen *Hamlet* as an appropriate object of inquiry. Not only has the play intrigued readers, audiences and critics in the sense we have just discussed: it also contains, in Hamlet's 'madness', the simulation – if not the actual experience – of mental illness. The first comprehensive attempt to produce a psychoanalytic explanation of *Hamlet* was made by an American psychoanalyst Ernest Jones, whose ideas – drawing on a note in Freud's *Interpretation of Dreams* – were first published in 1910.[3]

Examine these extracts from Jones's essay. What is the premise of his argument? and how does he explain the problem of Hamlet's 'delay'?

The whole picture presented by Hamlet, his deep depression, the hopeless note in his attitude towards the value of life, his dread of death, his repeated reference to bad dreams, his self-accusations, his desparate efforts to get away from the thoughts of his duty, and his vain attempts to find an excuse for his procrastination: all this unequivocally points to a *tortured conscience*, to some hidden ground for shirking his task, a ground which he dare not or cannot avow to himself .... The call of duty to kill his stepfather cannot be obeyed because it links itself with the unconscious call of his nature to kill his mother's husband, whether this is the first or the second; the absolute 'repression' of the former impulse involves the inner prohibition of the latter also.

Jones starts from the premise that Hamlet's obligation of killing Claudius is a plain and simple duty which Hamlet systematically and with great ingenuity avoids performing. The reason for that avoidance or 'delay' is never explicitly named in the play, though Hamlet is never short of circumstantial pretexts to justify his evasions. The real reason therefore, Jones argues, must lie in some 'hidden cause' concealed from the hero himself, invisible to the other characters, not evident even to the author of the play himself, but accessible to the techniques of psychoanalysis. Jones then proceeds to analyse Hamlet's condition in terms of the classic model of Freudian psychology.

DISCUSSION

Hamlet's hatred of his uncle is actually the instinctive hatred of a child for the father-figure, a reflex of the child's possessive sexual desire for the mother: Hamlet regarded his own father with enmity as a rival for his mother's affections. Such desires cannot be admitted to the conscious mind, and are therefore repressed, to return as psychoneurotic symptoms, and to inhibit the performance of any action resembling the desire itself. The disgust Hamlet feels towards his mother is occasioned by emotions arising from repressed sexual desire for her; his inability to kill Claudius occurs because the act is symbolically one of patricide, killing the father who is Gertrude's husband. Hamlet cannot bear to kill Claudius because the action would too closely resemble the wished-for murder of his own father. This classic Freudian interpretation produced much dissenting criticism, but remains important, and has been developed more recently by Jacques Lacan.[4] We will be discussing some of the problems that arise from it: such as Jones' unquestioned assumption that the obligation of revenge is to be taken as an unquestionable duty; the considerable distance that often appears between the surface meanings of the play and the 'hidden grounds' that attract the attention of psychoanalytic criticism; and the larger problem implicit in all theoretical criticism – is the play being recognised for what it is (which may be many things) or dissolved into the currents of a discourse foreign to its own particular language and artistic organisation?

III

Please return now to Act 1 scene i, and give it a careful reading with the following questions in mind.
(i) The ghost appears twice in this scene, and between its appearances the soldiers discuss the impending Norwegian invasion. What seems to you the relationship between this discussion and the supernatural apparitions?
(ii) Look again at Horatio's account of the duel between old Hamlet and old Fortinbras. What does the language of that description (1.1.80–95) tell us about old Hamlet?

(i) The relationship is one of analogy, is it not? Two kinds of invasion are occurring: the country is about to be invaded by a foreign power, and a parallel incursion into the mortal world is effected by the ghost.

Both invasions are the direct consequence of the killing of a king, and both are motivated by a desire for revenge and restitution. The parallel can be further extended, since there is much more emphasis on the 'warlike form' of the ghost's apparition, which corresponds to the military preparations described by Marcellus (1.1.70–9) – 'Such was the very armour he had on' (1.1.60); 'with martial stalk hath he gone by our watch' (1.1.66). If we missed the connection, Barnardo makes it explicit for us:

> Well may it sort that this portentous figure
> Comes armed through our watch so like the king
> That was and is the question of these wars. (1.1.109–11)

If we were to take the parallel further, we would discover that this relationship of analogy will hold only up to a certain point, beyond which it begins to prove deceptive. The external threat of the Norwegian invasion proves in practice to be an innocuous one, soon deflected by a little summit negotiation. The incursion of the ghost represents a more internal danger, since it points to corruptions and contradictions within the state of Denmark itself. If indeed 'something is rotten in the state of Denmark' then that internal weakness will prove far more intractable and perilous than the external threat of a military campaign.

(ii) You may well have found the language Horatio uses difficult, and have felt the need of explanatory notes: this is not surprising, since the passage contains many technical terms of a consciously legalistic and antique kind – 'a sealed compact, / Well ratified by law and heraldy', 'a moiety competent was gaged by our king', 'by the same comart / And carriage of the article design'. The language has proved quite obscure even to the professional commentators, though the general sense is clear: old Hamlet and old Fortinbras signed a detailed contract recording their mutual agreement that each would stake his kingdom on the outcome of the duel.

DISCUSSION

The linguistic effect of such archaic and specialised vocabulary is to isolate the action and differentiate it from the common language of the play's historical present: projecting the 'combat' back into a distinctively alien culture of the past. The two dead kings seem to occupy an ancient feudal society in which a passage of arms could be regarded as having great symbolic and even judicial significance. We have already observed that Claudius is a very different type of king: where old Hamlet would have ridden out to combat with Fortinbras, Claudius initiates negotiations. Young Fortinbras is also a different type from his father: he refuses to accept the legally binding contract by which Denmark annexed Norway, and gathers a private army to settle a personal and national grievance. Throughout the play we are given a repeated impression of a society very different from that heroic and feudal past: where young men are trained up as Renaissance courtiers rather than feudal warriors, where disputes are fought out by a game of fencing rather than a wager of battle. In place of the legally ratified combat of heroes we have the covert stabbing through the curtain, the secret plot of assassination, the poisoned cup and the envenomed foil; in place of the punctilious observation of legal codes 'well ratified by law and heraldy', we have the illegal rebellions of Fortinbras and Laertes, and the machiavellian diplomacy of Claudius.

Turn now to 5.1., and study it in the light of these questions.
(i) Consider the use of the word 'bound' in line 6. What does it signify?
(ii) What is Hamlet's immediate reaction to the ghost's injunction to revenge?
(iii) what emotions does the ghost express and convey towards the queen?
(iv) What do you understand by the word 'nature' in line 81? Use these two definitions from the *Oxford English Dictionary* to assist you: (a) 'a person's innate qualities or characteristics'; (b) 'general characteristics or feelings of mankind'.
(v) In what state of mind does the ghost leave Hamlet – decisive and resolute, or maddened by the experience?

(i) When Hamlet says he is 'bound to hear' the ghost, he may be expressing a mere willingness to listen, or a much stronger sense of moral and personal obligation.

DISCUSSION

Words like 'bond' and 'bound' derive from the vocabulary of feudal culture, and signify the complex of legal, moral, religious and traditional sanctions validating social and family relationships. In a feudal society a retainer or vassal was attached to a lord by a 'bond', sealed by a formal oath of fealty: the bond had a moral and emotional status as well as a legal force. In Shakespeare's England many of those feudal ties had disappeared or been radically changed, and the kind of comprehensive legal system with which we are familiar, in which all such relationships are defined and governed by law (contracts between employer and employee, legal obligations of parents to children, etc.) had only partially developed. In Elizabethan/Jacobean England the words had become to a certain extent specialised to the legal and financial associations they now carry.

There may therefore be a contest in this exchange between older and newer meanings. This view is supported by the ghost's response to Hamlet's use of the word: he is quick to appropriate and extend Hamlet's instinctive sense of indebtedness. Hamlet is 'bound' to do more than listen:

> HAMLET: Speak, I am bound to hear.
> GHOST: So art thou to revenge, when thou shalt hear.
>
> (1.5.6–7)

If Hamlet acknowledges the 'bond' of filial loyalty to his dead father and king, it is incumbent upon him to heed what the ghost has to say: but in the ghost's view that loyalty entails the binding moral obligation to take revenge.

(ii) Having been informed of Claudius' murder of his father, Hamlet has no hesitation in embracing the task of revenge and promising the ghost a speedy fulfilment:

> Haste me to know't, that I with wings as swift
> As meditation or the thoughts of love
> May sweep to my revenge. (1.5.29–31)

DISCUSSION

We might well find this passage confusing or even ironical: not only does Hamlet *not* sweep to his revenge with such precipitate haste, he actually appears to do the opposite – systematically and studiously avoiding the task. This problem of Hamlet's 'delay' has been much discussed. Earlier critics of the eighteenth and nineteenth centuries tended to look to inadequacies in Hamlet's character for reasons to explain the 'delay': while more recently critics have emphasised the difficulties involved in accepting the word of a ghost, and the obstacles standing in the way of a straightforward accomplishment of revenge which would involve killing a legitimate king.

The passage certainly seems to contain an element of 'dramatic irony', which can be focussed on the words 'meditation' and 'love'. It is surely no accident that they should appear here, given that the play characterises Hamlet emphatically as both an intellectual (eager to return to university at Wittenberg) and as a lover, who has been deeply involved in a courtship of Ophelia. The references here to 'meditation' and 'love' irresistibly draw our attention to the fact that Hamlet's revenge provokes in him (at least a pretence of) severe mental disorder; and comprehensively poisons and destroys his love for Ophelia. The phrasing of Hamlet's acceptance suggests a much more stable and unproblematical relationship between 'meditation', 'love' and 'revenge' than actually exists: as if the integrity of his whole nature can be thrown without difficulty into the task. But this portentous image of the meditative lover sweeping with decisive intellectual conviction and alert emotional readiness to a swift execution of revenge, gives way in the play to other images – the self-lacerating soliloquies of a vacillating melancholic, the 'wild and whirling words' of an ostensible madman, the disorderly and suspicious misogynist viciously violating a young girl's hesitant tenders of affection.

(iii) The ghost naturally exhibits towards Claudius his murderer a single-minded hostility, which is expressed in a language of forceful moral condemnation that echoes Hamlet's own (see above, pp. 39–40): 'that incestuous, that adulterate beast' (1.5.42). His attitude towards the queen is on the contrary not single-minded, but profoundly ambivalent.

DISCUSSION

Gertrude is perforce implicated in Claudius' moral offences – you can't commit incest and adultery on your own; had the queen been virtuous, she could never have preferred, over loyalty to her dead husband, the self-evidently inferior attractions of Claudius: but

> ... lust, though to a radiant angel linked,
> Will sate itself in a celestial bed,
> And prey on garbage. (1.5.55–7)

But there is an equally strong desire on the part of the ghost to exculpate Gertrude: Claudius is accredited with superhuman powers of seduction, 'witchcraft of his wits'. Yet the woman here excused can have been, in retrospect, only 'seeming virtuous' to be capable of yielding to Claudius' lust at all.

The ghost then has contradictory feelings toward his wife: and we may find this, given the circumstances, quite natural and psychologically inevitable – if ghosts are susceptible to the same rules of psychoanalytic judgement as those we apply to living people. The problem is that the ghost communicates a contradictory view of Gertrude to Hamlet too: on the one hand implicating her in the furious moral rhetoric directed at Claudius, a langauge conducive to extreme disgust, contempt and moral hatred; on the other hand expressing a chivalric protectiveness towards the queen, and enjoining on Hamlet an obligation of compassionate tolerance. Earlier Hamlet foreshadowed this courtly solicitude of his father –

> ... so loving to my mother
> That he might not beteem the winds of heaven
> Visit her face too roughly. ... (1.2.140–3)

And the ghost himself echoes his son's chivalric language:

> O Hamlet, what a falling off was there,
> From me whose love was of the dignity
> That it went hand in hand even with the vow
> I made to her in marriage ... (1.5.47–50)

The ghost's concluding admonitions reinforce this contradictory combination of moralistic contempt and considerate toleration:

> Let not the royal bed of Denmark be
> A couch for luxury and damned incest.
> But howsomever thou pursues this act
> Taint not thy mind, nor let thy soul contrive
> Against thy mother aught. Leave her to heaven
> And to those thorns that in her bosom lodge
> To prick and sting her. (1.5.82–8)

In respect of Claudius, the ghost places on Hamlet a single attitude and a simple responsibility – despise him, and kill him. In respect of Gertrude, the ghost places his son in what psychologists call a 'double-bind': in which a figure of authority (such as a parent) imposes on a dependent (such as a child) incompatible and contradictory obligations of equal force and validity. The ghost simultaneously excites Hamlet's imagination to a fervour of moral hatred against his mother, and insists that the emotion should be inhibited and withheld in favour of a loving exculpation of Gertrude's crimes.

(iv) 'Nature', like 'bond', is a keyword of Shakespearean tragedy, and a complex word in its own right – Raymond Williams has called it 'probably the most complex word in the language'.[6] Here it seems to contain some of its original meaning of 'born from' ('innate'): but there is something of the broader connotations of 'nature' to be found in the phrase 'human nature' – that which is 'natural' to human beings, those beliefs, feelings, modes of behaviour considered proper to members of the human community.

DISCUSSION

Although the ghost is talking about innate properties of Hamlet's character, he views those properties very much in terms of his own parental relationship to his son. At one level the ghost is saying: 'if you are my *natural* son (if Gertrude's adultery was not retrospective!) you will inevitably find this situation intolerable'; at another level he is invoking a larger conception of 'nature', and saying: 'if you possess the nature of a human being you are bound to recognise this as unbearable'. We have no reasonable doubt that Hamlet is not the ghost's natural son: but conceptions of what is 'natural' in terms of human feeling and behaviour are of course very much historical conceptions: they change from age to age and differ from society to society. The ghost's injunction to Hamlet forcibly asserts that a human being who is not in some way perverted, deficient or deformed in nature will instinctively feel the task of revenge to be a binding moral obligation. Yet such an assertion does not allow for the possibility that other conceptions of human nature might exist and require alternative patterns of behaviour: the Christian philosophy for example, which by Shakespeare's time had become the official ideology of the state, and which took a completely different line on revenge (see below, pp. 50–53). Notice also that the ghosts's syntax makes the inference from 'nature' into a command – 'bear it not' – rather than a logical deduction.

(v) The ghost leaves Hamlet in a state of powerful excitation and frenetic mental activity, which flows naturally into the assumed (or partially assumed) 'madness' he exhibits to his companions. But Hamlet is sufficiently collected to articulate a clear and decisive vow of revenge:

> Yea, from the table of my memory
> I'll wipe away all trivial fond records,
> All saws of books, all forms, all pressures past,

Which youth and observation copied there,
And thy commandment all alone shall live
Within the book and volume of my brain,
Unmixed with baser matter ... (1.5.98–104)

DISCUSSION

This is an appropriate response to the ghost's 'commandment',
exactly the sort of response it seems to have required. But the play
subjects that response to some sharp and pertinent questions. What
kind of mind is produced if one succeeds in deleting its entire
contents and programming it with one sole command? The answer
is partially given in Hamlet's own words: absolute obedience to
such a command produces a mind obsessively and monotonously
committed to the repetition of a single idea

O villain, villain, smiling damnèd villain! (1.5.106)

In fact, as you will be aware from your reading of the play, Hamlet
does not do this at all: his mind retains much of his previous
education and experience, neither of which he seems able
voluntarily to surrender. Whether that makes him a failure as a
revenger is a matter for further discussion.

IV

I want now to provide some information and provoke some debate
about the issue of revenge as it was understood in Jacobean
England, in order to give some historical context for our
understanding of its rôle in *Hamlet*. Obviously, we cannot know
what Shakespeare's personal view of revenge may have been, unless
that can be inferred from the plays – a procedure which in the light
of what has been said above, could well be regarded as impossible.
We can examine evidence about general attitudes towards revenge
in the late sixteenth/ early seventeenth centuries, and try to discover
whether or not there is a correct view which would elucidate our
reading of the play.

   Scholarly arguments about this issue can be divided into those
which regard revenge as a principle approved of by Renaissance
audiences; and those which hold that revenge was condemned and
deplored by those audiences and by the whole ethical system of the
society.[8] Arguments on the one side usually centre on theatrical
conventions, and the kinds of audience response likely to have been
aroused. When *watching* revenge plays, it is claimed, audiences
naturally accepted revenge as a form of justice, and as an

appropriate moral obligation upon the revenger. Although this conception of revenge was out of line with the dominant ethical system, Christianity, it existed in terms of theatrical experience, and was moreover supported by the survival within the society as a whole of a strong instinctive attachment to the revenge code. The nobility still believe, instinctively if not intellectually, in a chivalric code of honour under which revenge against personal injury or family dishonour had been a moral duty; and the old wager of battle survived outside the law in the practice of duelling. The common people still clung to the kind of vindictiveness of reprisal which had been common throughout the dynastic struggles of the later middle ages, and surfaced in assaults on racial minorities like Jews and Flemings.

On the other side of the argument scholars can marshall the evidence of contemporary judicial institutions, and contemporary Christian and humanist thought, to show that revenge was regarded in law as a crime, and universally condemned as a sin. A killing motivated by revenge was, under Elizabethan law, regarded as murder: it could be commuted to manslaughter only if the killing took place as a direct, unpremeditated reprisal against a serious personal injury (something like our concept of 'self-defence'). The most respected authorities of church and state were unanimous in their condemnation of revenge. Prosecuting a duelling case, Bacon argued that private quarrels could lead to family disputes, family disputes to public tumult, public tumult to national disorder. A homily 'against contention and brawling', expressing similar ideas, was appointed to be read in churches.[9] In ethical and religious terms revenge was regarded as a sin, rooted deep in the bestial and corrupt physical nature of man: the higher virtue was forgiveness, which emanated from the spiritual nature, and as a Christian virtue offered an alternative to the redemption of honour by rough private justice. The authorities of the state recognised revenge as an attempt by the individual to abrogate the state's power; and ecclesiastical authorities insisted that justice belonged to God: 'Vengeance is mine, saith the Lord: I will repay'. God could redress private wrongs through the workings of providence: while the revenger was a blasphemer who imperiled his own soul. Revenge was also condemned by physiologists as psychologically and physically damaging: the revenger would forget everything except his obsessive passion, which produced symptomatic ill-health and nervous disorders (see above, pp. 47–50). The dominant ethical system thus opposed revenge, and recommended in its place the virtues of forgiveness, patience, obedience, submission to the law and to God's will.[10]

Read the following passage, which is Francis Bacon's short essay *Of Revenge*, slightly cut.

> Revenge is a kind of wild justice; which, the more man's nature runs to, the more ought law to weed it out. For as for the first wrong, it doth but offend the law; but the revenge of the wrong putteth the law out of office. Certainly, in taking revenge, a man is but even with his enemy; but in passing it over, he is superior: for it is a prince's part to pardon. And Salamon, I am sure, saith, 'It is the glory of a man to pass by an offence'. That which is past, is gone, and irrevocable; and wise men have enough to do with things present, and to come: therefore, they do but trifle with themselves, that labour in past matters. There is no man doth a wrong, for the wrong's sake; but thereby to purchase himself profit, or pleasure, or honour, or the like. Therefore why should I be angry with a man for loving himself better than me? And if any man should do wrong, merely out of ill-nature, why? yet it is but like the thorn, or briar, which prick, and scratch, because they can do no other. The most tolerable sort of revenge is for those wrongs which there is no law to remedy: but then let a man take heed the revenge be such, as there is no law to punish: else, a man's enemy is still beforehand, and it is two for one. Some, when they take revenge, are desirous the party should know whence it cometh: this is the more generous. For the delight seemeth to be not so much in doing the hurt, as in making the party repent: but base and crafty cowards are like the arrow that flieth in the dark ... This is certain: that a man who studieth revenge, keeps his own wounds green, which otherwise would heal, and do well. Public revenges are, for the most part, fortunate; as that for the death of Caesar; for the death of Pertinax; for the death of Henry III of France; but in private revenges it is not so. Nay rather, vindictive persons live the lives of witches; who as they live mischievously, so their ends are unfortunate.[11]

Does Bacon seem to you to favour one side or the other in this debate? And can you see anything in his essay of relevance to Hamlet?

Bacon certainly appears to be squarely on the Christian-humanist side of the debate, offering a comprehensive condemnation of private revenge. But in fact the essay has been used as evidence on both sides of the modern scholarly quarrel about revenge: and a closer inspection shows it to be a focus of contradictory attitudes.

DISCUSSION

If revenge is a kind of 'wild justice', then notwithstanding the wildness it can apparently be regarded as a form of justice – as of course it originally was in earlier societies. Bacon acknowledges that revenge taken because of some failure of ommission or impotence of the law can be regarded as 'tolerable'; and that there is some virtue in revenge considered as a just punishment rather than a mere satisfaction of personal bloodlust. A revenger who wants his victim to repent can even be described as 'generous'. Finally Bacon offers an interesting distinction between 'public' and 'private' revenge, regarding the former as 'usually fortunate'.

There are numerous intersections with *Hamlet*, are there not? Bacon's use of the word 'nature' at the beginning contrasts interestingly with the ghost's: for Bacon is taking the Christian view that 'nature' is the wild, and unreclaimed element of humanity, which law, civilisation and religion need to 'weed out'. There is no law to remedy Hamlet's injury; his production of *The Murder of Gonzago* indicates that he wishes the king to be aware of his knowledge of the murder; and the killing of the king of Denmark must obviously be a matter of 'public' rather than 'private' revenge.

Bacon's essay seems to me an interesting analogy with the play. Arguing for a modern Christian-humanist view of revenge as immoral and anti-social, Bacon offers several qualifications, suggesting the need to accomodate revenge in certain circumstances. The play never seems to mention this modern view: yet since it was an immediate ideological context, it seems an improbable absence; and most readers agree that whatever *Hamlet* is, it is not an endorsement of the old revenge code. Both texts in their different ways perhaps register the complex and contradictory ways in which revenge was regarded in the society that produced them.

I will conclude this chapter with some brief guidance on intermediary scenes not discussed in detail. As I observed earlier, to search in *Hamlet* for a clear division between 'main plot' and 'sub-plot', or a sharp distinction between 'major' and 'minor' characters, is to embark on a complex and difficult task which may in the end prove not to be worthwhile. Is Polonius, for example, a major or a minor character? Do the scenes in which he appears occupy a 'main plot' or a 'sub-plot' position in the dramatic structure? Clearly he is not a major character in the sense that

Hamlet and Claudius are: yet he is apparently a leading figure in the court, he is directly or indirectly involved in much of the main action, and his accidental murder at Hamlet's hands is certainly a 'major' event of considerable significance and dramatic import. Again, how would we place the women in the play, Gertrude and Ophelia, in terms of such binary oppositions? Gertrude is surely a 'major' character, since much of the action depends on her: yet she remains an utterly passive figure, acted upon rather than initiating action; so it would be difficult to argue that she plays a major role. The fact that the women in the play are consigned to such passive positions calls for an explanation rather than a technical division into hierarchies of importance. There are a whole host of very minor figures, who play purely instrumental roles in the play: Voltemand and Cornelius, Reynaldo, Rosencrantz and Guildenstern, Osric. Yet these characters have their primary importance in relation to the self-evidently major figures; they tell us more about Hamlet and Claudius and Polonius than they tell us about themselves. Their minor status is in itself of major significance. Neither is it possible to split the play into dominant and subsidiary actions: for the simple reason that Hamlet himself elusively refuses to stay in one plot. The travelling actors and the gravediggers, who occupy the position of low-life 'clowns' in the play, are brought by Hamlet into the centre of the action; and the prince himself, as a consequence of his assumed madness and amazing verbal dexterity, constantly moves in and out of upper and lower-class worlds, dominant and subsidiary plots and scenes.

Look now at the following scenes and episodes: 1.3, 2.1, 2.2.1–40. Can you find any common theme or structure linking them together? And if so, what relevance does it have to the central action we have been considering so far?

The same thing is happening in each scene: a figure of authority is giving instructions to someone in a subordinate or subservient position.

DISCUSSION

First (1.3) we have Laertes instructing Ophelia to beware the advances of Hamlet; followed immediately by Polonius counselling the counsellor, and instructing Laertes to beware the attractions of France. Polonius himself then instructs Ophelia in much the same terms as those already offered by his son. Act 2 scene 1 shows Polonius instructing a servant to spy on his son, indicating how little he trusts Laertes to heed his paternal advice. Act 2 scene 2 shows the king instructing Rosencrantz and Guildenstern to spy on Hamlet. We might conclude then that 'instruction', together with 'espionage' and 'mistrust', are the themes linking these scenes together.

The application of these scenes to the main action is then that they consistently parallel it: since the inception of that main action is the instruction of the ghost to Hamlet. The knowledge of his father's murder confirms Hamlet's existing mistrust, and turns him into a kind of spy, constantly watching the king for proof and opportunity. Hamlet in turn had to instruct the soldiers and Horatio to observe an oath of secrecy (1.5.144), and the ensuing dialogue with those companions betrays a fundamental mistrust which never subsequently leaves him – the soldiers are of course theoretically loyal to Claudius.

Can we find in these intermediary scenes any further illumination of the main action? Work out for yourself how each recipient of instruction responds to the commands enjoined upon them.

There is a certain inconsistency and variation here, is there not? Ophelia for example accepts her brother's injunctions as advice – 'I shall th'effect of this good lesson keep' – and promptly turns his counsel back against him (1.3.45–51). By contrast she responds to her father with unqualified obedience: 'I shall obey, my lord'. (1.3.136) Laertes is completely non-commital about his father's instructions, practically ignoring them – 'Most humbly do I take my leave, my lord'. The scene between Polonius and Reynaldo is a comic parody, in which the servant agrees to obey some eight times, while his long-winded master still has more instructions to give. Rosencrantz and Guildenstern offer the king and queen complete and unqualified loyalty –

> But we both obey
> And here give up ourselves in the full bent
> To lay our service freely at your feet
> To be commanded.   (2.2.29–32)

DISCUSSION

How does this reflect on the ghost's instruction to Hamlet? Simply by indicating that people do not always precisely obey the instructions given to them by others: between the submissiveness of the court toadies Rosencrantz and Guildenstern and the sophisticated indifference of the independent Laertes, there are a range of variations in the way people receive instructions, understand them and act upon them. It is then perhaps less surprising that Hamlet shows considerable latitude in his interpretation of and submission to the ghost's command. At the same time these scenes present us with an atmosphere of espionage and mistrust, watchfulness and intrigue, which seems the characteristic tone of the Danish court. We also see evidence that figures of authority seek to exercise a despotic control over their subordinates, hoping to permit them as little liberty as possible. Does the ghost's command to Hamlet perhaps operate in the same way: imposing upon him as it does an unqualified and uncompromising demand for compliance, leaving no space for negotiation or difference?

Let us now reconsider and sift the findings of this chapter. We began with a comparison between Hamlet and Claudius, and discovered immediately that they cannot be comfortably assimilated into a simple moral pattern of hero and villain. The play makes available radically different responses to them, making possible a critical debate in which the respective qualities and rôles of king and prince can be disputed. It would probably be true to say that most *Hamlet* criticism casts Claudius as villain: but G. Wilson Knight was able to argue a diametrically opposite case:

> Claudius, as he appears in the play, is not a criminal. He is – strange as it may seem – a good and gentle king, enmeshed by the chain of causality linking him with his crime ... Hamlet is a danger to the state, even apart from his knowledge of Claudius' guilt.[12]

Most modern criticism attempts to accomodate this opposition by viewing Hamlet and Claudius as 'mighty opposites' linked in a deeply contradictory ethical and political contest.

This notion is supported by the play's emphasis on historical change: since the transition involved is not just from one monarchy to another, but a passage between two ethical systems. Our discussions of words like 'bond' and 'nature', and of Renaissance attitudes to revenge, have indicated that the play is very conscious of the ethical and ideological contradictions inseparable from historical change, and is continually revolving such concepts to make available different perspectives. When such historical changes take place with great rapidity, they can produce an atmosphere of serious moral crisis. Actions and beliefs that are valid within one political or ideological structure become invalid within another. Shakespeare's own age was no stranger to such changes, the principle one being the Reformation. A closer parallel to the play would be the fate of the feudal aristocracy, whose entire militaristic life-style became invalidated by the centralised Tudor nation-state.[13]

The heroic and militaristic world of old Hamlet, in which the revenge code was an unquestioned ethical obligation, is brought very close by the ghost to the more modern world of Hamlet himself: yet the historical reality of that world remains at a great distance, so that Hamlet is faced with the problem of enacting in fact the heroic deeds which are normally confined to fiction and fantasy; of breaking down the barriers between life and art, reality and legend.

This extremely problematical atmosphere helps to explain the pshchological complexity of the play, and its concern with the double significance of 'acting' as practice and performance. If we are commanded by an irresistible authority to undertake an action for which we have little or no personal or moral inclination, then that imposition is likely to have several results: we may resist or postpone the action; we may 'act' it by a kind of theatrical simulation, being seen to do what is required; and we may well find some considerable tension in ourselves between the internal promptings of morality or conscience, and the external imposition of authority. Is this not more or less what happens in *Hamlet*?

4. Madness and Metadrama

The principal theme of this chapter will be 'theatricality' – or to use a more modern critical term, 'metadrama'. These terms denote more than just the application of the play to specific theatrical conditions. They also concern the way in which the dimension of the theatre enters explicitly into the 'consciousness' of the play itself: where theatrical metaphors, and problems of acting, playing,

simulating, representing, become part of the play's internal
structure. We have spoken of how certain details of the play can be
performed in different ways in different theatres: we come now to a
deeper sense of the theatrical, and to the problems raised when, for
example, a separate play is performed within the play *Hamlet* itself;
or when the hero, by discoursing at length about acting and
theatrical representation and the moral powers of the drama, forces
us to be much more aware of the theatrical nature of the play
(Shakespeare's) which he himself occupies than we would be when
watching a completely naturalistic performance. *Hamlet* is, in other
words, to a degree 'self-reflexive': it offers itself to us, in certain
ways, as 'play' rather than 'reality': it encourages awareness of, and
reflection on, the mechanisms of its own production. Our primary
focus in this section will therefore be on the scenes in which Hamlet
appears with the players – 2.2 and the beginning of 3.2; his
soliloquy at the end of 2.2 (500–58, 'O what a rogue and
peasant slave am I!'); and the play-within-the-play itself, which is
formally entitled *The Murder of Gonzago* (2.2.491); although
Hamlet jokingly (and hoping doubtless to anticipate the popularity
of Agatha Christie) calls it *The Mousetrap* (3.2.216). Before going
on to discuss these scenes in detail, I will be offering a discussion of
Hamlet's 'madness', and some observations on the implications of
playing 'madness' in Elizabethan stage conditions. These matters
are not separate from the problems of theatricality, but rather at the
very heart of them.

Here is a series of quotations from various parts of the play dealing
with the issue of Hamlet's 'madness'. Study them now, and judge whether
or not it is possible to determine this issue in terms of a traditional
formulation: 'Is Hamlet really mad, or only counterfeiting madness'? Bear
in mind that 'ecstasy' could be a synonym for insanity, and that
'melancholy' was regarded as a psychological 'distemper' related to
madness.

HAMLET: As I perchance hereafter shall think meet
  To put an antic disposition on (1.5.171–2)

  I am but mad north-north-west. When the wind is
  southerly, I know a hawk from a handsaw. (2.2.347–8)

POLONIUS: To define true madness
  What is't but to be nothing else but mad? (2.2.92–3)
           I have found
  the very cause of Hamlet's lunacy. (2.2.49)

  Though this be madness, yet there is method in't.
  (2.2.200)

OPHELIA: Oh what a noble mind is here o'erthrown! (3.1.144)

CLAUDIUS: ... what he spake, though it lacked form a little,
      Was not like madness. There's something in his soul
      O'er which his melancholy sits on brood ...
      (3.1.157–9)

GUILDENSTERN: Nor do we find him forward to be sounded
      But with a crafy madness keeps aloof ...
      (3.1.7–8)

GERTRUDE: This is the very coinage of your brain.
      This bodiless creation ecstasy
      Is very cunning in.

HAMLET: Ecstasy?
      My pulse as yours doth temperately keep time ...

GERTRUDE: What shall I do?

HAMLET: Not this by no means that I bid you do.
      Let the bloat king tempt you again to bed ...
      Make you to ravel all this matter out
      That I essentially am not in madness,
      But mad in craft. (3.4.138–41, 181–3, 187–9)

Hamlet himself claims at different times to be completely rational, and to be simulating madness. Polonius thinks Hamlet is genuinely mad for the love of Ophelia: a view with which Ophelia and Gertrude both concur. Claudius suspiciously assumes Hamlet to be affecting madness to conceal some undisclosed motive; and his spies Rosencrantz and Guildenstern agree in this diagnosis of 'crafty-madness'.

DISCUSSION

One solution to the problem is to assume that Shakespeare followed his source directly, and gave Hamlet the kind of simulated insanity with which Amleth in the old story disarms the suspicions of his enemies. Hamlet himself seems to encourage this interpretation: he announces that he intends to 'put on' an 'antic disposition', as if the madness is a deliberately simulated disguise. He tells Rosencrantz and Guildenstern that he is only mad at certain times – i.e., he may be mad but he isn't stupid: though apparently raving, he knows what's going on. And by warning his mother not to betray him to Claudius he appears to acknowledge that his madness is a matter of 'craft'. That is certainly, as we might expect, Claudius' opinion: he is not convinced that Hamlet is genuinely insane, and suspects a hidden motive which the madness may be designed to conceal.

On the other hand there can be no doubt that for Ophelia Hamlet is absolutely and devastatingly insane: '… that noble and most sovereign reason/ Like sweet bells jangled, out of tune and harsh' (3.1.151–2). This is not simply because his behaviour is inexplicably odd, but because Hamlet shatters with violent ferocity the very quality of the understanding and communication that passed between them. The rupturing of that relationship, compounded by the subsequent killing of her father, throws her into an unmistakably genuine madness from which there is no escape. Polonius does not share Claudius' suspicion about the true cause of Hamlet's lunacy: he thinks Hamlet is mad for Ophelia's love. His phrase about madness with method in it might appear to suggest suspicion: but if you look up the context you will find that Polonius is merely musing that insanity has a strange logic of its own: and he characteristically adheres to his theory that the problem is 'the very ecstacy of love'.

The most difficult example is the piece of dialogue between Hamlet and Gertrude. There Hamlet claims a temperate rationality which his behaviour quite belies. We may believe, as Gertrude does not believe, that if we see a ghost it is reasonable to believe in its validity: so perhaps we do not acknowledge Hamlet's 'bend[ing] his eye on vacancy' (3.4.116) to be proof of a disordered imagination. Notwithstanding, Hamlet's language and actions can scarcely be described as rational: he has just killed Polonius, and proceeds to harangue his mother with an extraordinarily callous lack of interest in his former prospective father-in-law's corpse; and his address to his mother reveals not a cool rationalist but a man excited and inflamed with passions of hatred, revenge and jealousy.

This is not of course the only possible interpretation. If Hamlet kills Polonius in the mistaken belief that it is Claudius – 'is it the king?' – then he must feel, momentarily, that his revenge is accomplished: so it would be in embittered disappointment that he implies the victim deserved his fate. Similarly, if we take the characters and events of the play at Hamlet's own valuation, then the fierce moral rage he directs against his mother could be interpreted as a fair and appropriate reaction to her treachery and 'incest'. By the end of the scene he appears to be completely collected and reasonable.

On the other hand (3.4.182) by commencing his urgings with

'Not this by no means that I bid you do', Hamlet appears to be almost tempting Gertrude to incest and treachery, and exhibiting a perverse voyeuristic pleasure in the scenes of lust and betrayal his imagination conjures: 'Let the bloat king tempt you again to bed ...' (3.4.183). Although Hamlet may by deliberate act and decision choose to simulate madness, that does not necessarily mean that his true self is rational or sane: possibly the role of revenger does not allow for the preservation of reason, requiring as it does submission to a passion of violence.

We could perhaps say that at one level, the distinction between 'true' and 'feigned' madness will hold: and the reader or spectator can feel confident that the hero remains in control of his mind and imagination despite the erratic assumption of an 'antic disposition'. At another deeper and more psychological level however the distinction becomes more difficult to sustain, or breaks down altogether: the appearance of madness begins to look uncomfortably like insanity itself, and we find it increasingly difficult to locate amidst Hamlet's 'wild and whirling words' the cohesive core of integrity and reason he continually claims to possess.

Re-read the latter part of 2.1, paying particular attention to Ophelia's description of Hamlet's visit to her (2.1.75–98). What illumination does this throw on the problem of Hamlet's 'madness'? Is there any echo in it of an earlier part of the play?

Ophelia's description gives the impression of a deeply disordered mind and personality. If this is a dissimulation on Hamlet's part, it is an extremely effective one, and curiously motivated – why go to such lengths to persuade the innocent Ophelia of his mental alienation?

DISCUSSION

The line 'As if he had been loosèd out of hell/ To speak of horrors' inevitably recalls the apparition of the ghost, which claimed to emanate from purgatory, but certainly spoke to Hamlet of 'horrors'.

If we pick up that detail, the description begins to suggest that the influence of the ghost has converted Hamlet into a ghost ('pale as his shirt') in his own right; perhaps into what we would call the ghost of his former self. Initiated into the horrors of guilt and knowledge, Hamlet must bid Ophelia a reluctant farewell, the tenderness of their love 'blasted' by the harsh severity of the revenger's task. It could be argued that in truth Hamlet's resolution is firm and his integrity assured: the break with Ophelia is simply a particularly difficult and painfully emotional crisis which must be endured. The passionate intensity of his behaviour is then as Polonius diagnoses, an 'ecstasy of love'. Or if we assume that the madness is deliberately 'put on', we might well attribute to Hamlet a strategic motive: to preserve the secrecy of his purposes he cannot retain an intimacy with the daughter of his uncle's chief counsellor. Lastly there is the ambivalence of the descriptive medium itself: an incident reported, though by an honest eyewitness, is not the same as an incident seen: and we may well receive quite different impressions from the dramatic appearances of Hamlet himself.

Look now at the encounter of Hamlet and Polonius in 2.2.170–212. What kind of 'madness' does Hamlet exhibit here?

POLONIUS: Do you know me, my lord?
HAMLET: Excellent well, y'are a fishmonger. (171–2).

Madness with method in it, surely? Polonius' question, designed to test Hamlet's rationality, elicits the kind of answer he expects, a proof of insanity. The audience on the other hand is well aware that Hamlet is using the guise of madness to mock Polonius.

DISCUSSION

There may well also be a deeper meaning intended: 'fish' was a favourite focus of Elizabethan dirty jokes and bawdy innuendo: in this sense a fishmonger would be a purveyor of sexual favours, a pimp. As Polonius has in the lines immediately preceding this episode arranged to use his daughter as bait to snare Hamlet (2.2.160–4) – 'I'll loose my daughter to him' – the application seems entirely fair. This satirical undercurrent in Hamlet's speech surfaces later in the dialogue:

HAMLET: ... the satirical rogue says here that old men have grey beards, that their faces are wrinkled, their eyes purging thick amber and plumtree gum ...   (2.2.193–5)

This diatribe is too close to home to be anything other than deliberately intended: the 'satirical rogue' in question is Hamlet

himself. Our sense that Hamlet is play-acting here is confirmed ᴜ.
the entry of Rosencrantz and Guildenstern (2.2.213), when
Polonius leaves: the prince immediately drops his irrational disguise
and falls into an ordinary medium of conversation.

One other detail that should be noted is Hamlet's tendency to
speak in prose, which begins in this scene and remains throughout
the rest of the play a constant characteristic. The distinction in
Elizabethan plays between verse and prose was partly a class
distinction and partly a differentiation of genre: thus low-life
characters like clowns, shepherds, prostitutes, labourers would
speak in prose while their social superiors would generally adhere to
verse; and the proper medium for tragic and historical matter was
verse, while comic scenes would be conducted in prose. In speaking
prose, Hamlet is doing something unusual, eccentric and abnormal
from the point of view of dramatic convention. On the other hand
of course he is approaching closer to the ordinary language of oral
communication familiar to his audience from their everyday lives:
in distancing himself from the courtly formality of verse he engages
with the down to earth familiarity of prose. Thus when Hamlet
discourses in prose with the players or the gravediggers, he is
exhibiting both considerable linguistic flexibility and a striking
rapport with low-life characters and language. In addition Hamlet
is not only prosey in himself, but in several scenes he actually forces
other characters, against their own characteristic preference and
practice, to speak prose. Here (2.2.203) Polonius also breaks into
prose; subsequently Claudius is forced – reluctantly, it seems, and
with an explicit disavowal of the very language he is obliged to use
– to drop into prose in order to follow Hamlet's tone:

> HAMLET: I eat the air, promise-crammed. You cannot feed capons
> so.
> CLAUDIUS: I have nothing with this answer, Hamlet, these words
> are not mine. (3.2.84–5)

We will return to the links between prose and madness presently. First
read the 'nunnery scene', (3.1.28–182) considering these questions.
(i) In what context does Hamlet 'affront' (3.1.31) Ophelia? Does that
context influence our perception of his behaviour?
(ii) You may be using a text that indicates by stage direction that Hamlet is
aware of Claudius and Polonius watching the encounter. This is an
interpolated stage direction which has no basis in the Jacobean texts.
Do you think it a necessary or useful production device? How do you
think this scene would have been handled in the Globe playhouse?

(i) The scene begins with Rosencrantz and Guildenstern
diagnosing Hamlet's madness as 'crafty'. The meeting between
Hamlet and Ophelia is set up by Claudius and Polonius, who
proceed to spy on them: Polonius to ascertain if love is the cause of
the prince's lunacy, Claudius doubtless concerned to locate that
hidden motive over which Hamlet's melancholy 'sits on brood'.

DISCUSSION

A chance remark of Polonius' about the ostensible but deceptive
innocence of the instrument of their conspiracy provokes the first
definite indication of Claudius' guilt: 'How smart a lash that speech
doth give my conscience!' (3.1.50). (There is some doubt about the
textual authenticity of this aside, since it appears in only one of the
three Jacobean texts, the Second Quarto).[1] Prior to Ophelia's entry
Hamlet gives his 'To be or not to be' soliloquy, in which he
meditates on the pointlessness of existence and debates with himself
the alternative courses of suicide and action. It is characteristic of the
Renaissance theatre as a medium for so many things to be
happening at once: the action proceeds by a rapid series of
alternating and juxtaposed episodes rather than by long, fully-
developed and established 'scenes'.

How do we understand Hamlet's behaviour here, between the
apparently real insanity described by Ophelia in 2.1 and the
obviously assumed madness he shows to Polonius in 2.2?
Apparently surprised by Ophelia's entry, Hamlet addresses her in a
delicate and courtly style presumably characteristic of their
previous intercourse:

> Soft you now,
> The fair Ophelia. – Nymph, in thy orisons
> Be all my sins remembered.   (3.1.88–9)

That opposition between the idealised purity of the woman and the
incorrigible sinfulness of the man is the basic structural opposition
of the 'nunnery' speech (119–26): though the distinction made
quickly collapses into a reversed opposition in which the sexual
treachery of women makes 'monsters' of men (131–40). The
movement of Hamlet's language is from idealised courtly
compliment, through riddling satire, to bitter and self-
contradictory invective. If this is pretended madness, it is very well
played: for in its lacerating self-division, its obsession with sexual
guilt and innocence, violation and purity, its emotions of fear and

disgust directed towards female sexuality, it seems not dissimilar to the symptoms of genuine madness.

(ii) You may well have felt that a response to question (i) depends very much on a settlement of question (ii): knowing how carefully studied Hamlet's behaviour always is, we need to know whether or not he is aware that he is in the most literal sense 'th'observed of all observers' (3.1.148). If Hamlet knows that the king and Polonius are watching, then he may suspect Ophelia to be part of a plot, and his expressions can be a combination of resentment against her (the idealism of their love betrayed by her treachery) and veiled threats uttered towards the eavesdroppers – 'Where's your father? ... Let the doors be shut upon him' (3.1.126–8) for Polonius; and for Claudius 'Those that are married already, all but one shall live ...' (3.1.141–2).

It is common stage practice to let Hamlet catch sight of the concealed spies at one point or another in the scene: so that from that point his behaviour becomes explicable in terms of his attitude towards the king and those who conspire with Claudius. In a naturalistic performance such a question would have to be resolved by directioral decision: the actor must either show that he is aware of the spies or simulate ignorance; the spies would have to be properly concealed in order for Hamlet's discovery of them to have any point. In the Tony Richardson film discussed earlier (see above, p. 14) a particular camera-angle coupled with a reaction-shot of Hamlet informs the audience that he has seen his observers. How would this have been played at the Globe? As indicated earlier (see above, p. 26) concealment on the bare platform stage may have been purely nominal, its form enacted and its significance determined by convention. The presence of the witnesses as observers and spectators is thus directly present to the audience's minds without Hamlet ostentatiously spotting them. If the question 'does Hamlet see them' is governed by stage convention (i.e. the actor can see them but the character cannot) then the problem of his awareness can be left ambiguous. Perhaps Hamlet sees them, perhaps not: perhaps Hamlet is aware/unaware of the eavesdroppers as he is aware/unaware of the audience in the theatre. The fertile uncertainty of such a dramatic situation enriches the psychological and verbal complexity of Hamlet's speeches to Ophelia. Madness and sanity, guilt and innocence, knowledge and ignorance, the involuntary and the intended: in the open and diversified medium of the Renaissance public playhouse such antitheses could never have held firm and absolute, but must have performed an exciting and sometimes bewildering dance of opposition and inversion.

An important consequence of this originating theatrical context is that the state of 'madness', which we understand to be a condition of psychological derangement of varying degrees of severity, is more likely to have been understood in the Renaissance theatre as a particular repertory of rôles with corresponding dramatic possibilities. The position of the 'fool' in Renaissance drama is an analogous case: the word could denote both mentally subnormal individuals and clever, sharp-witted hired clowns: yet the fools of theatrical tradition seem to identify and to partake of both types. The deep structural relationship of 'folly' with 'madness' is intensively interrogated in a central scene of *King Lear*, (3.4) wherein a king driven mad by disillusionment, a licensed fool, and a dispossessed nobleman posing as a lunatic, participate in a crazy cacophonous dialogue of wisdom and folly. The actors who played 'clowns' in Renaissance plays were the great comedians of the day, some of them (such as Richard Tarleton and Will Kemp) more famous than many a forgotten tragedian. Such actors would satirically mime the stupidity of the true fool or enact the acerbic wit of the professional comedian, probably within the same scene of a play. There could be no exact correspondence or 'fit' between actor and character: the actor would move rapidly from one kind of role to another. In Shakespeare's English 'fool' was thus a double-edged term like our modern 'clown': we can use it pejoratively to attribute qualities to a person, 'clownish' behaviour: or to denote a particular type of professional performer. A 'clown' is a stupid or clumsy person, but a 'clown' is also a highly skilled professional entertainer.

The question 'is Hamlet mad?' might in this context be considered analogous to the question 'is the fool stupid?'. We know that the fool can 'act' both stupid and clever: and that behind both actions is a skilful technician and quite probably a highly intelligent consciousness. Similarly, Hamlet can 'act' both madness and sanity: but what kind of inclusive consciousness lies behind these enacted roles must remain elusive and mysterious. Is it an integrated centre of self akin to a human personality, which we might hope to fathom and understand? Or is it rather an actor, aware that the personality of Hamlet exists only in the roles provided for him, seeking to bestow conviction on each role in turn, but always maintaining a certain aloofness and distance, never allowing reader or audience to 'pluck out the heart of [his] mystery' (3.2.331)?

The kinship between Hamlet and the clowns has already been mentioned, and is particularly close for a Renaissance tragedy. Hamlet not only seeks the company of 'clowns' like the players and the gravediggers: he also seeks to appropriate their professional skills, showing the actors how to speak, instructing them in how to act, upstaging the gravedigger by taking over his patter of cemetery jokes. In all these aspects Hamlet distinguishes himself from the nobility and power of his principal role as the wronged prince of Denmark. In his madness, whether real or feigned, he exercises the kinds of verbal freedom and imaginative liberty employed in the Elizabethan theatre by both madmen and clowns to dissolve and restructure rigid heirarchies of significance and convention; and is able to move and switch flexibly and erratically between a bewildering variety of languages, tones, roles. His kinship with clowns gives him access to further regions of imaginative liberty and topsy-turveydom. Lastly, his association with professional actors foregrounds in the most decisive way, the question of his true 'identity', and the problematical nature of the drama itself.

Give a careful reading to 2.2, lines 500–558. How does Hamlet link the scene's preoccupation with drama to his duty of revenge?

Put simply, Hamlet is reproaching himself for being unable to perform the act of revenge: while a mere 'player' can simulate such intense passion for a fictional character, he himself can 'say nothing' (2.2.521). But the whole speech is also a complex play on the metaphors of drama and acting, characteristic of the Elizabethan theatre's self-conscious awareness of the peculiar nature of the theatrical experience.

DISCUSSION

There is a deep ambivalence, as we have already noted (above, pp. 38–9) in the theatrical vocabularly: I have just used the phrase 'to perform the act' of revenge, meaning to do the deed – yet both words also denote the kinds of action and performance just given artificially by the player.

The player's absorption in his role is described by Hamlet as a 'fiction', a 'dream of passion': dimensions of artifice and unreality, bearing no relation to the actor as a person or to his own life-situation, yet capable of engaging the emotions and producing a convincing simulacrum of practical 'action'. He then contrasts himself:

> What would he do
> Had he the motive and the cue for passion
> That I have? He would drown the stage with tears,
> And cleave the general ear with horrid speech ... (2.2.512–5)

Instead of taking the actor's simulated passion and transferring it to the domain of real action, Hamlet places himself (as he did earlier in the scene, 410–22) in the position of an actor, with a 'motive' and a 'cue' for passion. His image of himself and the figure of the player fuse, and he imagines himself *acting* (in the theatrical sense) so as to communicate to an imagined audience the chastening horror of his knowledge.

The persuasive and communicative power of the actor is contrasted with Hamlet's own sense of impotence:

> Yet I,
> A dull and muddy-mettled rascal, peak
> Like John-a-dreams, unpregnant of my cause,
> And can say nothing –   (2.2.518–21)

'John-a-dreams' is usually glossed as 'a dreamy person'[2]: yet it is likely that Hamlet is thinking of masturbation or nocturnal emission, a sterile climax ('peak') which leaves everything 'unpregnant'. The actor in his 'dream of passion' can infect others with emotion, while Hamlet can 'say nothing' (2.2.521).

Prompted (another theatrical metaphor!) by the actor's example, Hamlet attempts to master and exploit a dramatic language of revenge:

> Bloody, bawdy villain!
> Remorseless, treacherous, lecherous, kindless villain!
> Oh vengeance! (2.2.532–4)

Attempting to break into 'action' (in the practical sense) Hamlet finds he can only 'act' (in the theatrical sense) the conventional role of revenge hero. He summons the violent language of the old revenge play to his aid: but then breaks off in a gesture of disillusionment and self-disgust:

> Why, what an ass am I!   (2.2.535)

For a moment Hamlet seems to be consciously and overtly acting the role of a traditional revenge-play hero, swearing vengeance in the melodramatic style of an older (and perhaps in 1600 old-fashioned) dramatic genre. Suddenly he stops, steps aside from that role, and comments on it: the consequent break or discontinuity has the effect of throwing the revenge convention into relief, exposing its particularity of language, drawing attention to it as discourse, holding it up for the inspection of the audience's curiosity. Seeking for the possibility of action, Hamlet finds only acting: for the role of revenger itself is a theatrical convention, and in the very act of uttering his passion of revenge the actor collides with the conventional forms provided for such utterances. This

entanglement in the apparent inauthenticity of acting induces
Hamlet to decry the same dramatic power he has just envied:

> ... this is most brave
> That I the sonne of a deere murtherèd,
> Prompted to my reuenge by heauen and hell,
> Must like a whore vnpack my hart with words,
> And fall a-cursing like a very drabbe: a stallyon ... [3]

Here the role of actor is thrown into a different perspective, and
evaluated with a puritanical contempt for mere artifice and
simulation; Hamlet compares himself to a 'drab', a prostitute, who
is like the actor a paid performer, simulating passion in the
inauthentic artifice of her trade. A 'stallyon' is a male prostitute: I
have preferred the Second Quarto reading here, (the other texts give
'scullion') since the image of the prostitute is clearly an important
analogy with the actor.

We would imagine that at 2.2.595 Hamlet has distanced himself from the imitative superficiality of drama and is prepared
by self-chastisement for genuine action. The resolution that follows
may then be somewhat surprising: for Hamlet decides, not to kill
Claudius, but to direct a play. His motive for doing so – 'to catch
the conscience of the king' – is perfectly valid; yet such ensnaring
and demonstration formed no part of the ghost's original
commands. Conscious of that, Hamlet has to express doubts about
the authenticity of the ghost itself – doubts which have not
previously troubled him and which read here like invented pretexts.
To the ghost the moral obligation of revenge was the authentic
expression of a man's 'nature': for Hamlet it has the inauthenticity
of a role imposed on him from outside. Bear in mind however that
some critics, as we have already seen (above, p. 46) regard this
disquiet about the reliability of the ghost as wholly justified, since
Elizabethan religious beliefs were very conscious of the slippery
elusiveness of supernatural visitors. Other modern critics have seen
the ghost as symbolic of a radical uncertainty at the heart of the
play.[4]

It is not surprising that Hamlet should find himself unable to
escape from this trap whereby every attempt at action founders on
the sense of inauthenticity associated with acting: since he exists in
a medium in which 'Hamlet' can have no reality unless an actor
presents him. What this soliloquy – together with other devices
such as the introduction of a troupe of actors, the foregrounding of
theatrical activity, the play-within-the-play – succeeds in doing, is
to call attention to Hamlet as an actor, and to foreground the
particular dramatic conventions through which he is playing. In

this respect the play is operating not dramatically, but *metadramatically*. Metadrama is drama which deals not just with the elements of a story or dramatic narrative – the killing of a king, the hero's vow of vengence, the plotting and espionage of a corrupt court – but also with itself: it is self-reflexive, drawing attention to the artifice of its own construction, foregrounding the mechanisms of its own presentation. The play-within-a-play inevitably has this effect: the audience in the theatre finds itself watching another audience watching another play, which is evidently neither more nor less a constructed artifice than the play *Hamlet* itself.[5]

This characteristic of Shakespearean drama has been neglected by literary criticism, which often brings to such drama predominantly naturalistic methods of reading. Much literary criticism of a more traditional kind looks to drama, as to all literature, for the verbal articulation of authentic 'character' and 'experience': and where such realistic characterisation is not in evidence, finds the material itself wanting.

Read the following passage of critical analysis by L. C. Knights.[6] How does it relate to the preceding discussion? Does it echo some of the opinions expressed by Hamlet himself?

> Hamlet's habitual tendency is to make everything, even what he deeply feels, into a matter of play-acting. Again and again intrinsic values, direct relations, are neglected whilst he tries out various rôles before a real or imagined audience. He dramatizes his melancholy – for he insists on his suit of inky black even whilst denying its importance – just as he dramatizes his love and fall from love and his very grief for Ophelia's death; his jests and asides imply an approving audience 'in the know' and ready to take the point; he is fascinated by the business of acting (and highly intelligent about it) and he falls naturally into figures of speech suggested by the theatre ... Before the last scene the note of sincerity is found in few places except some of the soliloquies and the intimate exchanges with Horatio.

In Knights' view Hamlet is constantly neglecting the values he ought to be concerned with ('intrinsic values', 'direct relations', 'sincerity') in favour of a series of rôle-playing improvisations, which are here implicitly criticised as insincere, indirect and extrinsic to the self. The idea that activities such as acting, dramatization, rôle-playing and theatrical reference, conducted entirely within the medium of a *play*, should be the legitimate object of moral objection, may seem an odd one: but it is after all only an echo of Hamlet's own opinions.

DISCUSSION

What we see here is a literary critic discussing a play on the basis of the assumption that 'play-acting' is identical with the unreal and the inauthentic. But it is only by converting the play into a representational psychological novel that such a distinction can be made at all: for once this verbal text has been translated into the living medium of theatre, it becomes no longer possible to regard 'acting' as something essentially false and illusory, as a way of disguising the true self. 'Acting' is the very medium through which the play communicates itself to us: no actor, no Hamlet.

In our own century the theatre has been strongly influenced by the kind of literary-critical approach employed by L. C. Knights, and also by such influences as the naturalistic theories of Konstantin Stanislavsky, and the overwhelmingly naturalistic modes of film and television. Certain theatrical conventions can be used to construct the play as an exercise in psychological realism, in which the actor playing Hamlet never acknowledges that he is in reality an actor: but seeks rather to delude us into believing that he is the Prince of Denmark. Of course such theatrical 'illusion' always involves a certain internal distantiation, since we know that the actor is not a historical character, but a performer representing one. Nonetheless acting is very widely thought of in terms of 'authenticity' in the representation of psychological reality: the practice of reviewing theatre in newspapers and magazines, and on radio and television, consists very largely of critics evaluating performances in terms of their 'convincingness' or 'truth-to-life'. Such an emphasis tends to play down or completely occlude the kind of metadramatic self-reflexiveness characteristic of a play like *Hamlet*: which is continually forcing the actors and the dramatic medium itself into visible relief.

L. C. Knights' accent of contempt for the theatre and for dramatic illusion is prominent in Hamlet's own soliloquy: though full of admiration for the player's ability to simulate emotion, when Hamlet thinks of himself as an actor, he speaks the characteristic language of anti-theatrical propaganda, comparing himself to a whore. He attempts to sustain a distinction in which the real business of life is 'action', while acting in the theatrical sense is a mere 'fiction' (both artifice and deception), a 'dream of passion', a form of masturbation. Yet Hamlet is able to say things to an audience only when an actor is prepared to be the heart-unpacking whore, the cursing 'stallyon', to bring us a represented image of the Prince of Denmark. This contradiction – between the sharp, puritanical contempt for 'fiction' and the sterile pretences of actors; and a powerful respect for the capacity of drama to represent reality and to effect a moral transformation in its audience – lies deep in the play, deep in the theatrical culture of the age, and is actively foregrounded by the metadramatic medium of *Hamlet*.

    The ideas I have been discussing, and the view of drama I have been promoting, are deeply influenced by the theory and practice of Bertolt Brecht, and also by developments in literary criticism since the 1970s (see below, pp. 84–5) which have tended to question the very concept of art as an imitation of reality, and to celebrate in works of art those qualities which emphasise the distance between art and life.[7] This is not however at all the same thing as claiming that art is a purely 'aesthetic' experience unrelated to the practical problems of everyday living. That kind of drama, and that kind of criticism, are simply more concerned than their traditional counterparts to expose those tendencies in art that operate to serve or endorse particular cultural and political ideologies; and more concerned to promote the kind of art that is self-questioning rather than naturalistic, since the latter appears to accept the world as it is: while the former is more interested in the possibilities for changing it. (See Further Reading.)

    I have posed my reading of *Hamlet* against the kind of traditionalist literary criticism that seems to me to neglect the theatrical dimension and to privilege the literary form. It would however be an oversimplification to leave the debate there, since the emphasis on theatricality in the play can be acknowledged and yet taken to quite different conclusions. After all the Elizabethans found it quite natural to use the theatre as a metaphor for life itself – 'All the world's a stage' – and some of them may, for all we know, have recognised the internal world of a play, with its emphasis on role-playing, dissimulation, the untrustworthiness of appearances, as an imitation of life more accurate and truthful than the reassuring platitudes of contemporary ideology. It is certainly true that in our own time more sophisticated forms of literary criticism have accepted the metadramatic qualities of *Hamlet*, and concluded that it is in those very qualities of interrogative and self-reflexive play that the drama approaches most closely to an imitation of life. Here are two quotations arguing that view, taken from impressive critical essays which you would find rewarding to read as a whole. Study these on your own, and try to work out how each critic sees the relationship between theatricality and the imitation of life.

In this play as in many other tragedies, the experience of the
protagonist is not the deployment of a determinate character, but
the assumption, and then the enactment, of a determinate rôle. Rôle
predominates over character, because once it is assumed by an
actor, it will be much the same whatever his nature may be. It
overrides that nature: the play is its acting out … We have a
recognizable kind of situation, a man engaged in a known
career.[8]

Shakespeare's favourite terms in *Hamlet* are words of
ordinary usage that pose the question of appearances in a fundamental form. 'Apparition' … 'seems' … 'put on' and 'shape'. The
shape of something is the form under which we are accustomed to
apprehend it … but a shape may also be a disguise − even, in
Shakespeare's time, an actor's costume or an actor's role … 'Put
on' supplies an analogous ambiguity … Hamlet has put an antic
disposition on, that the king knows. But what does 'put on'
mean? A mask, or a frock or livery − our 'habit'? The king is left
guessing, and so are we …

We need not be surprised that critics and playgoers alike have
been tempted to see in this an evocation not simply of Hamlet's
world but of their own. Man in his aspect of bafflement, moving
in darkness on a rampart between two worlds …[9]

I would like you now to take a closer look at some of the
episodes involving theatricality, in the light of the above discussion.
I will offer some questions to guide your explorations, and brief
discussions against which you can test your own findings. The
Notes and Further Reading will point you on your way to further
work on this topic.

(i) Read 2.2.385−500. Compare Hamlet's views on drama with the following
passage from Sir Philip Sidney's *Defence of Poesie* (1595), in which Sidney
attacks the kind of theatre Shakespeare wrote for. How do the two passages
compare? and how do they relate to the theatre *Hamlet* was performed in?

Where the stage should always represent but one place, and the uttermost
time presupposed in it should be, both by Aristotle's precept and common
reason, but one day, there is both many days, and many places, inartificially
imagined …
… you shall have Asia of the one side, and Afric of the other, and so
many other under-kingdoms that the player, when he cometh in, must ever
begin with telling where he is, or else the tale will not be conceived …
But besides these gross absurdities, how all their plays be neither right
tragedies, nor right comedies, mingling kings and clowns, not because the
matter so carrieth it, but thrust in the clown by the head and shoulders to
play a part in majestical matters with neither decency nor discretion, so as
neither the admiration and commiseration, nor the right sportfulness, is by
their mongrel tragi-comedy obtained.[10]

(ii) Read 3.2.1–36. What do you think of Hamlet's theory of drama? How could his reference to 'the groundlings' (i.e. those spectators occupying standing positions in the yard) have functioned in the Globe theatre? The following argument by John Dover Wilson attempts an explanation of this relationship between text and audience: do you find it convincing?

> Hamlet is the greatest of popular dramas, and has held the stage for three centuries just because of that. Yet it is also full of 'necessary points' for which 'barren spectators' had no use, but which its creator was most anxious that clowning and overacting should not be permitted to obscure for the judicious. There is, for instance, Hamlet's quibbling, much of it, with double or triple point, beyond the comprehension of even the nimblest-witted among the groundlings. Its existence proved that Shakespeare could count on a section of the audience at the Globe, nobles, inns-of-court men and the like, capable in swiftness of apprehension and sustained attention of almost any subtlety he cared to put them to ... The quibbles did not worry the prentice-boys, because they, like many modern editors, took them as the nonsensical utterances of a madman; but the longer the judicious pondered them the more they found ...[11]

(iii) Consider 3.2.237–45. Does *The Murder of Gonzago* achieve its desired effect?
(iv) Study Hamlet's speech at 3.3.73–98. What do you make of his reasons for not killing Claudius?

(i) Hamlet and Sidney seem to share a common language of objection to the normal conventions of the public theatre: each expresses a dislike of dramatic disunity and unruliness of form, and a distaste for the intrusion of comedy into serious dramatic contexts, the uncontrolled comic liberty of the clown. Hamlet expresses a preference for a kind of academic drama uncontaminated by the theatre: a play so fine that 'it was never acted'. The curious thing is that *Hamlet* is a very characteristic example of the 'mongrel tragi-comedy' of the public theatres, quite unbounded by rules and notions of form, and full of interpenetrations between tragedy and comedy, the mingling of kings and clowns.

DISCUSSION

The kind of neo-classical dramatic theory espoused by Sir Philip Sidney used the teachings of Aristotle and the examples of Greek and Roman drama as models of what theatrical writing should aspire to: and insisted on the principles of form, rule, discipline, measure, decorum. This critical tradition was quite alien to the practices of the Elizabethan public theatres, whose bare unlocalised stages observed no unities of time or place; and quite antipathetic to contemporary theatrical writing, which drew eclectically on foreign and native traditions, and worked on principles of unity and coherence (see below, pp. 93–4) quite different from the classical sense of order. The dramatic theory Hamlet expresses here belongs to the neo-classical theory which was to a considerable attempt directed against the practices of the popular public theatres for which Shakespeare always wrote.

(ii) It seems curiously inappropriate to its theatrical context: an actor obeying every principle of Hamlet's dramatic theory would simply not be able to play the rôle of Hamlet. And when we 'read' the detail about the vulgar tastes of the 'groundlings', it is salutary to remember that when those words were acted the group thus maligned were tightly packed around the stage! Dover Wilson was confident that the play operated on two educational levels, one for the 'judicious' and the other for the 'groundlings': he simply endorses Hamlet's academic and élitist view. We may believe that the apprentice at the Globe would not have understood all the play's verbal subtleties: but can we believe that he received in respectful and submissive silence a series of direct insults to his taste and intelligence?

DISCUSSION

Hamlet's advice to the players has been taken almost universally to be Shakespeare's advice to his spectators: as the author's own dramatic creed. To accept the speeches on those terms is to take no account of their dramatic context: it would be curious to hear 'bloody, bawdy villian!' 'pronounced trippingly on the tongue', or 'now could I drink hot blood' spoken so as to 'o'erstep not the modesty of nature'. Such observations must have been a joke shared with the audience, and would therefore have worked to distance Hamlet into the assumed role of a neo-classical critic of the drama, laying down the law within the medium of a play whose dramatic form violated every canon of neo-classical criticism. Hamlet himself is constantly speaking 'more than is set down for him' by the ghost, and while in *The Murder of Gonzago* the players seem to abide by his instructions, *he* constantly interrupts and intervenes in the play to elaborate it and mediate it to the audience.

(iii) If we assume that the desired effect was to 'catch the conscience' of Claudius in the sense of provoking remorse in him, then 3.3 shows that that effect is achieved.

DISCUSSION

But Hamlet seems thereby to be no further advanced in his cause, and still avoids killing Claudius when he finds him praying. If on the other hand the object was to trap Claudius into openly revealing his guilt, to 'proclaim his malefactions' (2.2.545), to transfer the whole issue of the king's guilt from the murky shadows of a revenge plot to the open daylight of public justice, then the attempt seems to be a failure: Hamlet knows what he knew before, and no-one else seems any the wiser. It is worth observing that the Jacobean texts give no indication as to how 3.2.240–5 should be played: for example (Folio text):

> OPHE.   The King rises.
> HAM.   What, frighted with false fire.
> QU.   How fares my Lord?
> POL.   Give o're the Play.
> KING.   Giue me some Light. Away.[12]

Compare this with an edited version, John Dover Wilson's 1934 text:

> [*the king, very pale, totters to his feet*]
> OPHELIA.   The king rises.
> HAMLET.   What, frighted with false fire!
> QUEEN.   How fares my lord?
> POLONIUS.   Give o'er the play.
> KING.   Give me some light – away!
>   [*he rushes from the hall*]
>
>   (3.2.265–9)[13]

Where the Jacobean text leaves interpretation open, the modern editor has interposed between text and reader to obtrude a definite interpretation, in which punctuation and interpolated stage directions are used to confirm what the original text refuses to divulge – whether or not Claudius is shocked into revealing his guilt. There are many other ways of saying 'Give me some light. Away' (see below, p. 79); and it appears that Shakespeare left such decisions to his fellow actors. The problem left unresolved is one of the most intractable problems of cultural theory: can art have a beneficial moral effect on the spectator? Hamlet's experiment proves inconclusive.

   (iv) 3.3.73–96. is a very difficult moment. It is the point at which Hamlet has an apparently heaven-sent opportunity to kill

Claudius. In fact he avoids the issue by expressing the extraordinarily violent and cruel desire to kill Claudius in an act of sin so that he may go straight to hell.

DISCUSSION

Since Claudius is in an attitude of prayer, and since we have been initiated into the moral struggles of his soul, we might expect Hamlet to refrain from killing him out of religious scruple or moral sensitivity. But here Hamlet's language is once again the crude and violent language of the revenge convention – 'up, sword, and know thou a more horrid hent' – which hitherto he has regarded only as a rôle he can assume, not a desire he can embrace. We are forced to conclude that Hamlet the character is *acting* here: but whether that performance expresses or conceals his deeper motives remains a mystery.

These aspects of *Hamlet* have been registered in many different productions: indeed it is arguable that they constitute so decisive a feature of the play's dramatic structure that they could hardly be excluded from a performance situation. I would like to introduce you to one production which was distinguished by the application of a sustained consciousness of *Hamlet* as a metadramatic work: John Barton's Royal Shakespeare Company production of 1980.[14] Barton had previously shown an interest in the metadramatic potentialities of other Shakespeare plays, at least in terms of characters (such as Richard II) who appear to adopt the qualities of actors: and the theoretical dimension of the 1980 *Hamlet* apparently owed more than a little to his wife, who twenty years earlier as 'Anne Righter' had written one of the first monographs on Shakespearean metadrama, *Shakespeare and the Idea of the Play*.[15] The programme for this production printed passages from Anne Barton's introduction to the New Penguin Shakespeare edition of *Hamlet*, published 1980, under the heading of a phrase from the play, 'actions that a man might play', to clarify and draw attention to the production's theoretical basis:

> Shakespeare had often, in the plays he wrote before *Hamlet*, considered the nature of poetry, the imagination, and the actor's art. *Hamlet*, however, is unique in the density and pervasiveness of its theatrical self-reference ... The tragedians of the city who arrive so opportunely at Elsinore in Act II provide a focus for extended disquisitions upon acting, and for two inset plays. The

stage imagery of *Hamlet*, however, exists independently of the professional actors who appear in Acts II and III. It is there from the beginning, and it remains important in the final movement of the tragedy ... When the First Player weeps real tears for the fictional sorrows of Hecuba, Hamlet is reminded by them of how thin the dividing line can be between life and art ... what Hamlet does not reveal to the players is his private, and more unorthodox understanding of how art may acquire a temporary and upredictable dominion over life: how dramatic fictions can comment upon the situations in which individual members of the audience find themselves in ways far more complex and disturbing than any mere exemplary tale.[16]

Some of the techniques the production employed to foreground this aspect are described here by Michael L. Greenwald.

The RSC stage, as rendered in Ralph Koltai's simple design, contained its own stage: a slightly elevated, gradually raked platform turned at an angle towards the audience. This conspicuously artificial stage-on-a-stage was surrounded by benches which became a *theatron* for the spectators *in* Elsinore's unfolding drama: the Court watched the king and his minions perform their ceremonial functions in this Danish theatre-in-the-round; in 4.4. crazed Ophelia arranged her audience around this stage to enact her bawdy incantations while seated on the prop throne used earlier by the Players; the Hamlet-Laertes duel – for which the antagonists wore masks (fencing headgear) – found the contrived stage a natural space for this last 'maimed rite', an event Anne Barton descirbes as germane to the revenge genre: 'a fictional action, performed by selected characters before an unsuspecting on-stage audience, explodes without warning into real, as opposed to mimic, destruction'.[17] And finally it was this stage-upon-the-stage to which four captains bore the dead body of Hamlet to place it in a pool of light for the final tableau, the logical conclusion of Barton's concept.[18]

As you can see from this description of the staging, the production aimed at the kind of non-illusionistic flexibility of the Elizabethan public playhouse stage itself, which always, whatever the kind or degree of illusion aimed at in the playing, appeared to be nothing more nor less than a theatre. Such a stage could similarly keep the audience constantly aware of the theatricality of the event, and thus provoke a constant cross-fertilising dialectic between artifice and reality.

DISCUSSION

The most powerful moment of the production as I recall it was certainly the play-scene, in which Hamlet threw himself fully into the guise of an actor, wearing a multi-hued 'motley' cloak and brandishing a toy sword. Throughout the scene Hamlet was never still, constantly moving from one stage-area to another, in and out of the acting area of the play-within-the-play, and in and out of the prop throne placed opposite Claudius' real one. Claudius remained seated throughout, occupying a real, not simulated, throne. The conflict of antithetical kinds of power between the two 'mighty opposites' Hamlet and Claudius was enforced by the distinction between the restless chameleon Hamlet, seeking to exert the powers of fantasy and imagination through speech, gesture and drama; and the immobile form of the king, confident in the heavy inertia of effective political power. At the point where Claudius rises Hamlet had his theatrical sword pressed against the king's chest; Claudius in rising pushed Hamlet back, and uttered his line 'Give me some light. Away' in a tone of contemptuous indifference to Hamlet's theatrical posturings. Both the potentialities and the true impotence of cultural power when confronted with the duress of political sovereignty were evoked by this self-reflexive counter-arraignment of power and art.

I would like to recapitulate some of the issues we have so far discussed.
(i) Look carefully at Hamlet's short soliloquy "Tis now the very witching time of night', 3.2.349–60. How many of the topics so far considered does this speech bring into focus?
(ii) Examine the moment of the ghost's re-appearance at 3.4.101. What is the dramatic significance of its return at this particular moment?

(i) *Revenge*: Hamlet is speaking the language of the revenge convention, and therefore expressing sentiments of melodramatic hatred quite out of keeping with his more intellectual and meditative disposition. The brutal savagery expressed seems even more out of place if we reflect that the 'bitter business' he embarks on is not the killing of Claudius, but a visit to his mother. That disparity suggests that we also have here the presence of an element of *metadrama*: Hamlet is 'acting' the rôle of revenge hero, assuming a character that is not his. But the violent emotions directed against his mother – the desire to kill her ('my tongue and soul in this be hypocrites') are genuine enough.

The relationship between the desire to kill Claudius, the assumed role or accepted duty of revenge, and the intense moral hatred of his mother, is an extremely problematical one, and seems to call for the techniques of *Freudian analysis* (see above, pp. 40–43). Hamlet claims to *feel* the desire for revenge; yet in order to express it he has to *act* it. The deliberate assumption of a role presupposes that the actor is in control of the emotions thus evoked. Yet Hamlet's inability to separate his vindictive hatred of Claudius (who murdered his father) from his moral loathing of Gertrude (who didn't) suggests a nature in which contradictory emotions can find no integration or balance.

The word 'unnatural' can serve as a focus of these problems. Hamlet doesn't want to kill his mother, since that would be 'unnatural' – the crime of matricide would surely exceed Gertrude's offence of 'incest'. Yet Hamlet confesses to desiring that murder, which is surely unnatural in itself. But as we have seen the play problematises the concept of 'nature': the ghost would obviously regard such feelings as 'natural' if directed against Claudius, but as 'unnatural' if pointed at Gertrude. It is Hamlet's problem that in his 'nature' these distinctions have broken down, and the violence he should direct in action towards Claudius he directs in passion towards his mother.

(ii) Hamlet's immediate reaction is to assume that the ghost has returned to 'chide' him for permitting both opportunity and resolution to slip by (3.4.106–8); and the ghost confirms this:

> This visitation
> Is but to whet thy almost blunted purpose.

But the ghost seems at least as much concerned with Gertrude, and importunes Hamlet to comfort her: 'Speak to her, Hamlet' (3.4.114).

DISCUSSION

After all, the ghost only told Hamlet to do two things: to kill Claudius and to leave his mother alone. He has done neither. The ghost displays a chivalric protectiveness towards the queen which is perhaps in keeping with his feudal ideology, but certainly alien to the kind of bitter moral exhortation Hamlet has been engaged in. We might see this as an extension of the historical differences between old and young Hamlets: the prince sees no reason why a woman should be exempted from moral responsibility by a patriarchal chivalric solicitude. On the other hand, the seed of Hamlet's moralistic abuse is surely to be found in the language of the ghost himself, who originally confirmed his son's febrile loathing for the adulterous betraying woman. Hamlet can be seen as a sternly Calvinistic Christian humanist, insisting – in implicit defiance of the ghost's compassion – on the strict responsibility of the sinning individual for the state of her own soul. On the other hand we might feel that neither father nor son can effectively reconcile the emotional and ideological contradictions that assail them.

5.   Catharsis or Catastrophe?

We will now begin to approach the play's culminating catastrophe in 5.2, and to analyse its significance and dramatic impact. Our approach to that conclusion will involve a series of interpretative exercises on various intervening episodes. Act 4 of *Hamlet* has often been considered a disorderly and unintegrated area of the play, in which the main thrust of the action seems to lapse and enter a long drawn out suspension until Hamlet's return to Denmark sets it back on course. In his absence the play focuses on the children of the murdered Polonius, the madness of Ophelia and Laertes' rebellion (e.g. 4.5.). It certainly appears that in the playhouse this section of the play was considered a candidate for cutting: the bulk of 4.4, in which Hamlet encounters the army of Fortinbras and delivers the soliloquy 'How all occasions do inform against me', does not appear in the Folio text, which gives only a brief episodic appearance to Fortinbras, probably to remind the audience of his existence prior to his final re-entry in 5.2. Bertolt Brecht thought that Act 4 of *Hamlet* was not a script to be played right through, but a series of *alternative* episodes from which the actors could choose and extemporise a complete action.[1] I would like you therefore to consider as we look at these episodes whether the text we are studying can be regarded as a perfectly integrated whole in which every part is indispensable and receives its significance from the unified whole. On the Jacobean stage *Hamlet* might have been a somewhat different 'whole' every season, every week, perhaps even every afternoon. In the light of that principle I will be proceeding through Act 4 by a series of brief interpretative discussions of particular scenes and incidents, followed by an intensive analysis of both scenes of Act 5.

Read 4.5. What is the point of this scene? What is Hamlet's attitude to Fortinbras' expedition? What light does the scene throw on Hamlet's problem of revenge?

As has already been indicated, there is a purpose in introducing Fortinbras briefly simply to recall his existence: otherwise the audience would not actually see him until the end of 5.2, and would doubtless wonder who the hell he was. The conversation between Hamlet and the captain, and Hamlet's subsequent soliloquy, serve to develop, however, an obvious contrast between Hamlet and Fortinbras, already linked as two parallel sons of slain fathers (see above, pp. 44–45). Hamlet thus appears to us – and to himself – juxtaposed into a relationship of contrast with a practical man for whom decisive action and military violence are as 'natural' as they were to old Hamlet. The contrast prompts Hamlet to reflect on his own inadequacies as a man of action and resolve.

DISCUSSION

Underlying the Norwegian campaign, we recall, is a son's revenge for his father's death: this same army was originally mustered to attack Denmark, though Fortinbras is apparently entirely content to deflect his military efforts to an unmotivated battle. Did you find it difficult to define Hamlet's attitude to the Norwegian campaign? In one sense the decisiveness of Fortinbras is a foil to Hamlet's hesitancy, one of the 'occasions' which 'inform against [him]'. If Hamlet could act with similar practicality and resolution, Claudius would already be dead. Yet despite its context of self-interrogation, the soliloquy is also a brilliant and incisive satire against the futility of military adventurism. The kind of 'honour' that thinks it noble to quarrel on such a scale over a straw or an eggshell is seen (both in the demotic commonsense of the captain and in Hamlet's sophisticated satire) as a ludicrous quality: an illusory form of vanity ('with divine ambition puffed') that thinks nothing of sacrificing 20,000 men for a patch of ground hardly big enough to bury the corpses of the fallen. Simultaneously then Hamlet is proposing Fortinbras as an admirable example of heroism to be emulated; and as a ludicrous parody of heroism to be satirised. Far from resolving or simplifying Hamlet's problems, this speech seems to compound them: the final resolution to think nothing but 'bloody' thoughts, sustained only by a meditation on the self-defeating paradoxes of action, rings hollow – as hollow as Hamlet's earlier adoption of the revenger's role on the strength of an actor's performance.

At least these gestures ring hollow if action is truly – as Hamlet seems to believe – the desirable end. Our problem is that the Hamlet who shows more enthusiasm for a cultural activity such as directing a play, for a humanistic effort such as offering moral exhortation to a sinner, or for a vigorous exercise in anti-military satire is a peculiarly modern figure by comparison with those 'examples gross as earth' who cling to antiquated principles of honour and revenge. And our problem is analogous to the problem that must have been encountered by the original audience: since in manifesting that kind of interest in the humanistic activities of culture and morality, Hamlet represented something of the essential spirit of the Renaissance itself (though it could certainly be argued that Claudius represented other equally important aspects;).[2] Is Hamlet interesting and attractive to us precisely to the extent that he does not immediately fulfil the ghost's command? Does he compel our curiosity not as a revenger, but by virtue of those actions he undertakes as *alternatives* to revenge?

Give a careful reading to 4.5, considering the following questions:
(i) Look at the 'Gentleman's' description of Ophelia's madness (4.5.10–13). What general preoccupations of the play are invoked here?
(ii) Ophelia is clearly very much changed by her breakdown. List some of the ways in which her dramatic role is now different from her previous appearances.
(iii) Laertes' appearance at the head of a rebellion (4.5.110–52) is clearly intended as a variation on the theme of a son's response to the murder of a father. How does Laertes' example compare with other illustrations in the play?

(i) Madness, of course: but also the *meanings* of madness, the peculiar ways in which nonsense can sometimes signify more than sense.

DISCUSSION

Ophelia's speech is in itself 'nothing' yet 'the unshaped use of it doth move/ The hearers to collection' – that is, the form of Ophelia's utterance, though impenetrable to ordinary logic, yet provides the hearer with opportunities for inferring meaning. The 'scholar' Horatio, with a concern for Hamlet's safety but with an additional vested interest in the stability of meanings and values, regards such indeterminate communication as potentially dangerous: 'she may strew/ Dangerous conjectures in ill-breeding minds'.

It was one of the conventions for representing madness on the Elizabethan stage that insanity could express deep and important truths (as Edgar puts it in *King Lear*, 'Matter and impertinency mixed! reason in madness!') though not by invoking what we think of as the normally stable relationship between the 'sense' of language and the 'sense' of an orderly and integrated vision of the world: meaning is implied and inferred rather than expressed in the extravagant fantasies of madness or the riddling aphorisms of its pretence. And here in the speech of an anonymous gentleman is a sophisticated theory of that form of communication; just as Laertes' speech at the end of the scene shows a remarkably modern understanding of the eloquence of silence, of the fact that a more powerful charge of meaning can be produced by the *absence* of ordinary signs of social signifying – in this case the rites of a state funeral for his father – than by the customary observation of those rites. This fertile curiosity about language is doubtless one of the qualities of Shakespearean drama that makes Terry Eagleton ironically suggest: 'Though conclusive evidence is hard to come by, it is difficult to read Shakespeare without feeling that he was almost certainly familiar with the writings of Hegel, Marx, Nietzsche, Freud, Wittgenstein and Derrida'.[3]

Such aspects of the play naturally make it of enormous interest to contemporary deconstructionist and other forms of 'post-structuralist' criticism, since they are themselves rooted in a theory of language which denies any fixed or stable relationship between language and what language denotes or signifies. Terry Eagleton, one of the critics who has applied such criteria to Shakespeare, collects a number of related contexts together in this characteristically brilliant formulation:

> [Hamlet] spends most of his time eluding whatever social and
> sexual positions society offers him, whether as chivalric lover,

obedient revenger or future king. As fluid as his father's ghost and as fast-talking as any Shakespearean clown, Hamlet riddles and bamboozles his way out of being definitely known, switching masks and sliding the signifier to protect his inner privacy of being against the power and knowledge of the court.[4]

'Switching masks and sliding the signifier': you can see a relationship there between the kind of metadramatic approach we have been considering, and the approach based on post-structuralist concepts of language.[5]

(ii) This question may seem a simple one: previously Ophelia was sane, now she is mad. Her previous behaviour was always proper and formal, the cultivated perfection of a well-mannered court lady; even under the stress of great emotion, she never departed from the controlled eloquence of a measured verse. Now even her formality can appear uncertain and riddling in its meaning: her line 'Where is the beauteous majesty of Denmark' may be a courtly compliment, or (especially juxtaposed to the queen's aside about her 'sick soul') a poignant elegy for lost innocence (4.5.16–21); and her usual mode of speech is now an 'antic' prose interspersed with snatches of popular song.

DISCUSSION

If we look more closely at Ophelia's utterances, on the assumption that 'This nothing's more than matter' (4.5.173), we will find beginning to emerge some deeper meanings, and a different way of defining the contrast between Ophelia before and after. Two particular points seem of importance: the fact that her ramblings harp on her treatment at the hands of Hamlet as well as her father's death; and the element of bawdy sexuality in the popular songs she sings. Consider this as a contrast:

> O what a noble mind is here o'erthrown!
> ... And I of ladies most deject and wretched
> That sucked the honey of his music vows,
> Now see that noble and most sovereign reason,
> Like sweet bells jangled, out of time and harsh ...
>> (3.1.144, 149–52)

> By Gis and by Saint Charity
>   Alack, and fie for shame!
> Young men will do't if they come to't
>   By Cock, they are to blame.
>> (4.5.58–61)

A simple antithesis of 'sanity' and 'madness' will not adequately encompass this change: for it is also a transition from the abstract idealism of courtly sentiment to the earthy world of popular song, in which – for the first time – Ophelia can confront the facts of sexuality directly. Consider the phrase 'sucked the honey' in that first context: the lyrical abstraction of 'music vows' robs it of any possibility of the sexual innuendo that is normally very close to the surface in verse of this period: whereas in the song, 'By Cock' is unmistakable in its *double entendre*. The change in Ophelia is also one from repression to liberty: from the constrained and rarified abstractions of courtliness to the liberated openness of popular speech and song.

Madness is for Ophelia a personal tragedy: but it is a tragedy that discloses the vulnerabilities and internal weaknesses of the society that holds her in such repression that insanity is the only means to freedom, the only access to the open world of common experience. It is in this respect that the play can deliver meanings – about the position of women in society, and in their relationships with fathers, lovers and husbands – of interest to feminist criticism. But here also feminist criticism meets one of its perennial and most intractable problems: to appropriate the play for a feminist cultural politics, it is necessary to foreground the specifically female experience of the play, and to give to the women characters the same kind of emphasis traditionally accorded to the males. It is abundantly obvious, as we have seen, that the play relegates women to a distinctly subordinate role, so that a focus on their experience will risk the charge of distortion; of paying a disproportionate attention to subordinate meanings. Feminist criticism would argue that in this respect traditional literary criticism operates in an ideological and political way to approve and endorse a structure in which masculine experience and priorities appear as dominant; to simply accept this structure would be to accept the marginalization and oppression of the feminine. It seems to me that the play presents and exposes with sharp clarity the victimised and subordinate positions of women in Hamlet's society, forced both to bear the violence and irresponsibility of male power, and to carry the burden of masculine guilt (I can see no other convincing reason why such an emphatic role should have been given to Ophelia, who is clearly incidental to Hamlet's tragedy) so that one could argue that the play's vision is itself feminist. On the other hand the play contains some very powerful anti-feminist rhetoric, especially in Hamlet's own language – 'Frailty, thy name is woman!' – and if we were to accept Hamlet's own observations as generally valid, then the play would be communicating a misogynist view of women as treacherous, untrustworthy, lustful, given to cosmetic deception and better off in a nunnery. I do not think we need to accept or endorse Hamlet's own views at all: but any feminist argument needs to negotiate the difficult terrain of misogynistic sentiment abundantly in evidence in the play. Feminism has no choice but to interrogate the play overtly in the light of contemporary political and cultural considerations: to read it, in Walter Benjamin's phrase 'against the grain'[6] of its own apparent ideological emphases. To an extent feminist criticism has led the way for much modern criticism in thus openly acknowledging its political project.[7]

(iii) Laertes is much more like Fortinbras than he is like Hamlet: immediately on hearing of his father's sudden death, he arrives from France with an army. Similar conduct by Hamlet at the time of old Hamlet's death would presumably have resulted in the overthrow of Claudius.

DISCUSSION

Everything Laertes says about revenge throws him into sharp contrast with Hamlet. 'That drop of blood that's calm proclaims me bastard' (4.5.118) indicates that Laertes' 'nature' contains the instinctive desire for revenge that the ghost expected to find in Hamlet. Laertes' adoption of the language of revenge tragedy is quite different from Hamlet's in being apparently genuine and uttered with the utmost sincerity:

> To hell allegiance, vows to the blackest devil,
> Conscience and grace to the profoundest pit!
> I dare damnation. To this point I stand,
> That both the worlds I give to negligence,
> Let come what comes, only I'll be revenged
> Most throughly for my father.
>
> (4.5.131–6)

Laertes appears capable of that complete evacuation of mind unsuccessfully attempted by Hamlet (1.5.98–104, and above, pp. 45–50): he can renounce everything except the desire for revenge.

I asked in that earlier context what kind of character Hamlet would become if he did succeed in thus emptying his mind of everything but revenge. The answer is given indirectly by what happens to Laertes. Read 4.7 with that point in mind. If the play encourages us to develop a sustained comparison between Hamlet and Laertes, what are the results in this scene?

Laertes seems very unlike Hamlet in his capacity for singleminded commitment to revenge; and perhaps even more unlike in his vulnerability to manipulation. For this scene is surely an example of how the singleminded man can be drawn under the control of an unscrupulous man of greater subtlety and complexity of awareness.

DISCUSSION

The case Claudius makes to Laertes seems at one level both reasonable and politically expedient: if the order of the realm is indeed bound up with the security of the king, and if the presence of an unruly prince who refuses the appropriate social integration threatens that security, then what else can Claudius do but proceed against Hamlet? Assent to Claudius' proposals presupposes however not only acceptance of those premises, but endorsement of the consequences which follow from such a machiavellian assumption: that is, that proceedings against Hamlet need not take the form of open judicial process or political negotiation, but can be managed by covert conspiracies of treachery and betrayal. Hamlet's popularity and Gertrude's love for him (4.7.9–24) inhibit Claudius from any overt assault on him; but the king has no scruple about adopting a procedure which might effectively circumvent those obstacles. The language Claudius uses here is that of machiavellian rule:

> I will work him
> To an exploit, now ripe in my device,
> Under the which he shall not choose but fall,
> And for his death no wind of blame shall breathe,
> But even his mother shall uncharge the practice
> And call it accident. (4.7.62–7)

Laertes' response seems to suggest complete indifference to these subtleties of scruple and inhibition: revenge is for him the overriding principle which occludes consideration of any other value: 'My lord, I will be ruled' (4.7.67). If you recall our earlier discussion (above, pp. 54–57) of relationships between authority and service, Laertes appears to be one of those prepared to offer complete subservience – and in this respect too he contrasts with the Hamlet who consistently denies and rejects absolute obedience to instruction or command. Once Claudius can rely on this pliability, backed up by a little courtly conversation and flattery of Laertes' qualities (4.7.80–104), the king can offer Laertes his objective – revenge – in exchange for what he himself wants – the death of Hamlet.

Please read 5.1, considering the following questions.
(i) Compare the way in which the gravediggers (called in the Jacobean texts 'clowns') discuss Ophelia's death with the queen's reported narrative at 4.7.163–83. What kind of contrast is this? And what is the dramatic impact of the queen's account?
(ii) Sir Philip Sidney complained that the theatre of his day violated dramatic decorum by mixing high and low matters, 'mingling kings and clowns'.[8] What disparate things are mixed in this scene?
(iii) What echoes do you find in the encounter of Hamlet with the gravediggers of earlier details of the play?
(iv) What do you make of Hamlet's intervention into Ophelia's funeral service? Given that he has been discussing death in the abstract, ignorant of Ophelia's suicide, does he now behave in a manner more appropriate to the interment of his former lover?

(i) A very sharp contrast, certainly! The two contexts offer diametrically opposed attitudes towards the significance of Ophelia's death: one elegiac, idealised, lyrical, couched in an elaborately mannered, almost antique style; the other ironic, scurrilous, satirical:

> Her clothes spread wide,
> And mermaidlike awhile they bore her up,
> Which time she chanted snatches of old lauds
> As one incapable of her own distress,
>
> (4.7.175–8)

OTHER: The crowner hath sat on her, and finds it Christian burial.

CLOWN: How can that be, unless she drowned herself in her own defence?

(5.1.3–5)

DISCUSSION

I think it would be a mistake to set these two accounts into a 'hierarchy of discourses', regarding one as dominant and the other as subordinate: the queen's (main plot) account being the correct one, and the clown's (sub-plot) version a kind of ironic deviation – a mere interlude of 'comic relief' to leaven the dominant tragic tone. As I indicated earlier (above, pp. 53–57) a stable division between main and sub-plot cannot really hold: the tones of the play shift with great rapidity, largely as a consequence of the flexibility and fluidity of Hamlet's character, but also because such rapid alternation of scenes was the natural rhythm of drama on the bare stage of the Jacobean public playhouse. Within such a continuous but hugely diversified and variegated flow, it is difficult to believe that an audience could or indeed should feel secure about who is a main and who is a subsidiary character, whose discourse is dominant and whose subordinate, whose opinions should be regarded as of importance and whose relegated to the category of 'light relief'.

The style of the queen's elegy for drowned Ophelia involves a theatrical technique which is in its way just as 'distancing' as the professional mockery of clowns: the long narrative speech of reported action, derived from the classical theatre, in which scenes thought impossible or improper to be acted were reported by an eyewitness. The queen's account is not even eyewitness (or, we assume, she might have made some attempt to restrain Ophelia from taking the plunge), and its slow, self-consciously poetic, rather precious style is entirely inappropriate as a vehicle for the transmission of urgent and important news.[9] On stage a speech like this changes the quality of dramatic 'time', making it obviously very different from 'real time'. The beautiful idealism of the queen's memorial tribute makes the death of Ophelia into a myth, suitably embodied in Millais' famous pre-Raphaelite painting. But myth is by definition not reality: so Gertrude's account is no more valid or true than that of the clowns.

The discourse of the clowns is a ritualised comedy of death, which knows no piety, no inhibition, no moral sensitivity: it devours everything and reproduces it as humour, with the promiscuous appetite of death itself. Do we feel this language, following hard upon the queen's poignant elegy, to be cruel, heartless, 'unnatural'? That is a possible response, perhaps more likely on the page than in the theatre, where the saturnalian energy and wit of the clown seem to be an irresistible provocation to laughter. It seems to me more likely that we can respond with the same degree of commitment to both dramatic discourses: leaving us with a repository of contradictory responses which the play may or may not ultimately resolve.

(ii) The prince's colloquy with the gravediggers is an obvious example of that 'mingling kings and clowns' regarded by Sidney as a violation of dramatic propriety (see above, pp. 73–5).

DISCUSSION

As we observed in an earlier discussion (above, pp. 66–67) the play actually secures an affinity between prince and clown, with Hamlet speaking much the same kind of language as the gravediggers (notice his immediate shift from prose to verse when the funeral procession approaches – 5.1.184) so that the firm social distinctions upon which neo-classical dramatic theory based its principles begin to dissolve. The scene consistently draws attention to similar juxtapositions of things conventionally regarded as separate or contradictory, such as death and comedy:

> HAMLET: Has this fellow no feeling of his business? A sings in grave-making. (5.1.66) ... That skull had a tongue in it, and could sing once (5.1.76) ... the age is grown so picked, that the toe of the peasant comes so near the heel of the courtier, he galls his kibe (5.1.42–44) ... Here hung those lips that I have kissed I know not how oft (5.1.189–91) ... Imperious Caesar, dead and turned to clay/ Might stop a hole to keep the wind away. (5.1.215–16).

(iii) I would list the gravedigger's songs, the references to Cain, the terms 'politician' and 'courtier', and the diatribe against feminine artifice.

DISCUSSION

The gravedigger's song recalls the kind of popular ballad sung by Ophelia in her madness. The queen paid an appropriately formal and idealised tribute to Ophelia's sanity; the clown pays a corresponding tribute to her madness. The pre-Raphaelite Ophelia who floated singing on the water's surface, and the 'poor wretch' who sank to 'muddy death' (4.7.182–3) appear to be contradictory aspects of the same woman.

Hamlet observes that the clown treats an exhumed skull 'as if

twere Cain's jawbone, that did the first murder' (65): the Biblical fable
of fratricide had already occurred to Claudius as a parallel to
his own crime: 'It hath the primal eldest curse upon't/ A brother's
murder' (3.3.37–8). 'The pate of a politician ... that would
circumvent God' (66–7) is likely also, given the proximity of 4.7, to
put us in mind of Claudius, whose skull Hamlet would like to
handle in earnest rather than jest. The satirical image of the
'courtier' (69) might recall from the same preceding scene Laertes
with his talk of courtly skills, horsemanship and fencing. A deep
dramatic irony operates prospectively as well, since both the
characters alluded to are to meet Hamlet in death in the subsequent
scene.

Hamlet's address to Yorick's skull on the mortality and artifice
of women ('get you to my lady's chamber, and tell her, let her paint
an inch thick, to this favour she must come', 163–4) recalls the
'nunnery scene' ('I have heard of your paintings, too, well enough',
3.1.137) and Claudius' comparison earlier in the same scene of his
own guilt to 'The harlot's cheek, beautied with plastering art'
(3.1.51). Hamlet's account of the processes of decomposition will
perhaps recall his earlier lecture to Claudius on 'how a king may go
a progress through the guts of beggar' (4.3.28–9).

(iv) Hamlet's behaviour is surely very strange. Though he
protests that he 'loved Ophelia' (5.1.236) there is nothing in his
language or actions of tenderness, regret, guilt or any other of the
emotions that might be expected of him.

DISCUSSION

He seems to respond more directly to the histrionic grandiloquence
of Laertes, and is provoked to up-stage a man he immediately
marks as his rival:

> What is he whose grief
> Bears such an emphasis? ... This is I
> Hamlet the Dane ... What wilt thou do for her? ...
> Woo't weep, woo't fight, woo' fast, woo't tear thyself?
> Woo't drink up eisel, eat a crocodile?
>
> (5.1.221–243 passim)

What is Hamlet doing here? Expressing genuine grief for Ophelia?
Surely not, in that parody of heroic language. If it is Laertes'
extravagances of language and gesture he is parodying – 'Nay, and
thou'lt mouth,/ I'll rant as well as thou' (250–1) – it ill becomes
Hamlet to accuse anyone else of over-acting.

There are many possibilities of interpretation. If we assume that Hamlet is fully in control of what he is doing, then we have to assume that he is feigning madness (successfully – 'Oh he is mad Laertes', 5.1.239) and precipitating a situation that may take him closer to his revenge. The 'Hercules' in his parting couplet (5.1.258–9) may be the king, Laertes the cat who 'mews', Hamlet the dog who will 'have his day'. If we assume that Hamlet is the victim rather than the actor of violent emotions, then either he is less concerned with Ophelia's death than with other matters – his competition with Laertes, his revenge – or he is expressing grief for Ophelia indirectly, deflecting the violence of what could be self-destructive passion into other channels and against other people. Hamlet's own explanation of his behaviour here appears later, 'But sure the bravery of his grief did put me/ Into a towering passion'. (5.2.79–80).

We can now return to our starting point, and consider whether the dramatic narrative we have been following through Act 4 and the first scene of Act 5 is indeed a disorderly and unintegrated series of episodes which do not appear to have been consolidated into a single unified action. It is abundantly clear that every detail of the play we have examined has some relationship with its total structure – Hamlet's encounter with Fortinbras' army, Ophelia's madness and death, Laertes' passion of revenge and Claudius' manipulation of it, the explorations of death in the graveyard scene, can all be related to the central themes and abiding preoccupations of the play. At the same time, the fact that these details are all parts of a larger whole does not necessarily indicate that they are *indispensable* components of a perfect unity. Much literary criticism since the Romantic period has privileged the notion of a work of art as a complex but integrated unity, in which every part is subordinate to the whole, and the whole is the sum of its parts. A play like *Hamlet* can certainly be regarded in this light: but what happens to such a seamless totality when it is adapted for performance, and parts of it may be found dramatically ineffective, thematically unnecessary or simply too long? As I observed earlier (above, pp. 81–82) this area of *Hamlet* certainly was cut in performance on the Jacobean stage: and if we become too concerned with the concept of a play as a unified totality of indespensable elements, we are likely to think of the theatre as a medium which debases or adulterates the 'true' artistry of the play: 'the nearer we get to the stage, the further we are getting from Shakespeare'.[10] It was initially in the neo-classical criticism of the Renaissance, and then in a more compelling form in the Romantic criticism of the early nineteenth century (Charles Lamb, S. T. Coleridge) that a privileging of the 'organic unity' theory arose together with a revulsion from the plays in the theatre. It is surely the most absurd proposition that Shakespeare, who wrote for, acted in, and managed a theatre all his professional life should secretly have been working his way towards the nineteenth-century conception of the play as a *Gesamtkunstwerk*.

It follows that the metaphors of 'organic unity' which arose from that post-Romantic criticism are likely to be an inadequate technique for analysing a play like *Hamlet*. Each element belongs to the whole: but the whole can lose some of those elements and still function perfectly well as a play. A better critical metaphor, often used of *Hamlet*, is that of a system of parallels or a series of mirrors: Ophelia's madness and Laertes' revenge parallel and reflect Hamlet's madness and revenge, but the latter could still make sense, could still be played, without those parallels.[11]

Different scenes of the play accentuate different aspects of the whole, and what one interpretation will want to foreground another will want to omit. The episode in 5.2. between Hamlet and Osric can be regarded as an unnecessarily extensive piece of satire interpolated at a point where Hamlet and the audience are waiting for something decisive to happen. Again, this part of the scene was evidently cut in performance.[12] But this kind of comic satire against the affectations and absurdities of courtly and fashionable manners, besides having a contemporary popular appeal, undoubtedly has a legitimate place in *Hamlet*. If you wanted to develop this aspect, you would keep this episode; if you were more interested in focussing on Hamlet himself, or pressing on with the action, you would cut or omit it. The play will not die as a consequence of such an excision.

Now read 5.2, considering the following problems and questions:
(i) Consider Hamlet's narrative to Horatio (5.2.1–75). What aspects of Hamlet's character does this story reveal? What do you make of his attitude towards the deaths of Rosencrantz and Guildenstern?
(ii) Think about lines 62–70 in terms of the revenge theme. What do they tell us about its development?
(iii) What suggestions arise from the dialogue between Hamlet and Horatio at 5.2.185–96?
(iv) Do you think Hamlet's conciliatory and complimentary addresses to Laertes (198–230) are sincere or mocking?

(i) The narrative certainly reveals a man of considerable resourcefulness, courage, presence of mind: and above all, a man of action, who regards the fate of Rosencrantz and Guildenstern as well-deserved.

DISCUSSION

Hamlet's story is a miniature spy thriller in which he appears as a hero who exists on a level of intense physical sensation and who acts rather than thinks:

> Sir, in my heart there was a kind of fighting
> That would not let me sleep ... Up from my cabin,
> My sea-gown scarfed about me, in the dark
> Groped I to find them out, had my desire,
> Fingered their packet ...
>
> (5.2.4–15 *passim*)

Has Hamlet become the man of action he has always ambivalently emulated and despised? It would certainly seem so: though it is perhaps significant that this episode is narrated rather than dramatised – there is no reason why such events should not have been enacted – so there is again a certain distantiation, and we can therefore be aware that Hamlet is dramatising himself.

If Hamlet has become the man of action, is he to be admired for it? That question seems to me to raise a serious ambiguity in the play. Embroiled in and in peril of the espionage and conspiracy of Claudius and Claudius' henchmen, Hamlet finds himself counter-spying and counter-plotting in a way that makes him curiously like his enemies. We could argue that there is for him in this situation no other means of survival: but that cannot explain the peculiar quasi-sexual pleasure ('groped', 'had my desire', 'fingered their packet') Hamlet takes in penetrating Claudius' secrets. Horatio seems at least mildly surprised that Hamlet displays so little compunction in arranging the execution of his former friends: 'So Guildenstern and Rosencrantz go to't.' (5.2.56). But Hamlet insists that their fate is well-deserved:

> Why man, they did make love to this employment,
> They are not near my conscience. Their defeat
> Does by their own insinuation grow.
> 'Tis dangerous when the baser nature comes
> Between the pass and fell incensèd points
> Of mighty opposites.
>
> (5.2.57–62)

'By their own insinuation' indicates that by interposing between the 'mighty opposites', Hamlet and Claudius, the dispensable duo procured their own 'defeat'. Two aspects of the play emerge from this formulation. One is Hamlet's intensifying sense of himself as a 'scourge and minister' appointed to establish justice on earth. The other, related to that conception, is a notion of retributive 'poetic justice' which has been broached on several occasions earlier in play, and emerges towards the end of this final scene as a predominant pattern. When Hamlet kills Polonius he suggests that his fate is well-deserved: 'Thou finds't to be too busy is some danger' (3.4.33); and at the end of that scene he talks, apropos of Rosencrantz and Guildenstern, of what 'sport' it is 'to have the engineer/ Hoist with his own petar' (3.4.207–8). The concept of 'poetic justice' is of crucial importance to our understanding of the final catastrophe: suffice it to say that Hamlet is unlikely to endear himself to his audience by the callousness and aristocratic *hauteur* of what he says here.

(ii) The following speech has quite a different impact. Prompted by Horatio's expression of disgust – 'Why, what a king is this!' (5.2.62) Hamlet offers a list of Claudius' crimes as a justification of revenge. In thus openly appealing to a sense of public justice and the demands of private conscience, Hamlet indicates his own distance from the moral simplicity of the ghost's command, which required no such appeal or justification.

DISCUSSION

The speech is persuasive in form, addressed directly to Horatio; it is also clearly an attempt at self-persuasion; and at another level it is offered for consideration to the audience – Hamlet wants us, too, to be certain that Claudius' death is desirable for reasons other than the code of private revenge. This speech can even throw a retrospective light on all Hamlet's fore-going activities, which have – whether intentionally or not – resulted in this self-evidence of Claudius' guilt. At this point more than any other, it seems to me, Hamlet appears to have genuinely and sincerely integrated his task of revenge into some larger moral perspective. He feels also that he has little time: 'It will be short. The interim's mine' (5.2.73). It is perhaps all the more surprising therefore that he still does not kill Claudius, but accepts, with considerable misgivings, a challenge from Laertes – a man who has every reason for wishing Hamlet dead.

(iii) The apprehension Hamlet feels and very vividly expresses ('thou wouldst not think how ill all's here about my heart' –

185–6) is surely entirely justified, since he knows full well that Claudius and perhaps also Laertes are his implacable enemies. Horatio's advice is prudential: to trust such foreboding and withdraw from the duel. Is Hamlet's response heroic or suicidal?

> Not a whit, we defy augury. There is a special providence in the fall of a sparrow. If it be now. 'tis not to come; if it be not to come, it will be now, yet it will come – the readiness is all. (5.2.192–5)

(iv) Impossible to tell, surely? Earlier Hamlet expressed a convincing sympathy with Laertes: 'For by the image of my cause, I see/ The portraiture of his' (5.2.77–8). But his attendant phrase 'I'll court his favours' sounds a little ominous, especially in the light of the satirising of Osric. Before the duel Hamlet offers Laertes a rather extravagant display of courtesy, which prompts Laertes to suspicion: 'You mock me sir' (229). It seems to me inappropriate to prescribe a correct reading of this: whether we are reading, interpreting or producing, we have to elect choices and make decisions on such matters. Do we want Hamlet to appear impeccably noble, a chivalric youth putting his plotting adversaries to shame, almost innocent in his trusting frankness and scrupulous honour? Do we want him to appear much more machiavellian than that, fully aware of the danger he is in, responding to it with great intellectual resourcefulness, strategically acting the role of a conciliator, watching carefully for an opportunity to press home his advantage? On such decisions will rest the nature of our reading, our writing, our acting, our directing: the text will not tell us.

Give a close reading now to the rest of the scene.

(i) What additional instances occur of the notion of 'poetic justice'? Does it seem to you that the dénoument enacts such a pattern of retributive justice? Use the following passage from an essay by John Holloway to help you consider this question:

> In the end, it is not from Hamlet's rapier that [Claudius] dies ... but from the poisoned cup that he has himself prepared and that he has just tried to have passed to Hamlet ... As for the Queen, her death also comes, as retributively it should, in the intoxication and delight of the wine she has taken at the hand of Claudius. Laertes is the same. The rapier that he intends for Hamlet is that which kills him.[13]

(ii) Think about Horatio's lines 359–64. How do they illuminate our sense of the justice of the outcome?

(iii) It is often assumed that the closure of a Shakespearean tragedy shows the restoration of 'order' after rupture and disturbance. Does Fortinbras' arrival suggest that to you?

(i) There are several other instances of 'poetic justice':

LAERTES: I am justly killed with mine own treachery. (287)
            ... The foul practice
            Hath turned itself on me ... (297–8)
            ... He is justly served
            It is a poison tempered by himself. (306–7)

The concept of justice invoked here is one of simple retribution, identical in structure to the law of revenge: an eye for an eye, and a tooth for a tooth. The punishment should always be in exact proportion to the offence, a perfect symmetry of guilt and its reward.

Whether Claudius dies from Hamlet's rapier or his own poison the outcome is a symmetry of poetic justice: the life of a brother for the brother he poisoned, or death from the sword treacherously designed to kill his nephew. Laertes is killed by his own poison and his own sword, though he has already compensated for the death of his father by killing Hamlet.

DISCUSSION

But what of Hamlet and Gertrude? What justice is served by Hamlet's death, except that of revenge for Polonius? And can we really accept that Gertrude deserves to die: the innocent sensuous woman, guilty only in her compliance with the lusts of men? It would seem that the kind of justice operative here is not even the old simple revenge code, but a force more interested in symmetrical patterns than in fairness and equity: a poetic justice which has all the attractive shapeliness and perfection of art, but which can offer little assistance in the complex problems of assigning due punishment to human weakness and criminality.

(ii) The question stares us in the face: have Hamlet and the ghost between them succeeded in setting the world to rights, or rather in plunging it into chaos, wiping out the entire Danish royal family and allowing the state to fall into the hands of a soldier of fortune?

DISCUSSION

Hamlet is confident that 'the justice of his cause', if reported aright, will endorse and exculpate his actions. Horatio's hint as to what

kind of narrative that will be does not align with Hamlet's
self-righteousness. For what Horatio describes is a mess:

> So shall you hear
> Of carnal, bloody and unnatural acts,
> Of accidental judgements, casual slaughters,
> Of deaths put on by cunning and forced cause,
> And in this upshot, purposes mistook
> Fallen on th'inventor's heads.

(5.2.359–64)

Is Hamlet to be exculpated by this version of events? This list of
offences could well be applied to him: his 'accidental judgement' of
Ophelia, the 'casual slaughter' of Polonius, the 'deaths put on by
cunning and forced cause' of Rosencrantz and Guildenstern;
perhaps Hamlet's own death is to be regarded as one of those
'purposes mistook/ Fall'n on th'inventors' heads'.

(iii) The arrival of Fortinbras *is* a necessary restoration of order:
the ruling class of Denmark cannot go on indefinitely killing one
another. But it is also, surely, a final and bitter irony: since
although the ghost of old Hamlet may have been appeased in its
thirst for revenge, the old king's work is simultaneously undone. The
crown he asked his son to purify by cathartic violence now simply
reverts to that same foreign power the father had heroically
defeated.

DISCUSSION

Whether we approach the play's concluding scene through textual
analysis or through images of performance, the results are the
same: there can be no final or certain answer to the questions we
raise. Is that final scene a harmonious resolution or a disastrous
blood-bath? Does it exhibit a pattern of retributive justice
performed to the last letter of the law, or a chaotic orgy of
reciprocal slaughter in which the innocent fall aimlessly beside the
guilty? If the dramatic action performs a symmetrical pattern of
poetic justice, can it be both artistically satisfying and morally
acceptable? It is the play's insistent questioning that endures, not
the various answers that readers and critics and actors and directors
provide: even though, paradoxically, it is only in the formulation of
such answers that the play survives at all.

I would wish to close this study, therefore, not with some
apparently conclusive and authoritative summary, but with a small
sample of the many and varied voices that have spoken of *Hamlet*.

Read the passages, and compare the different approaches to the play. Notice how different they are, and yet each in its way persuasive and convincing: how easy it would be to find objections to each, yet how undeniable it is that each accurately draws attention to some recognisable aspect of the play. Notice above all how each critic seems to be talking as much about him/herself as about Shakespeare, so that speaking about *Hamlet* seems always to be a way of speaking about one's own contemporary world. That will be as true of what I have argued in this book as it it for any other critic: perhaps when we observe S. T. Coleridge offering what is obviously an engaging self-portrait passed off as a description of Shakespeare's character, we might take as a salutary warning that almost comic affirmation: 'I have a smack of Hamlet myself, if I may say so'.[14]

S. T. COLERIDGE

In Hamlet [Shakespeare] seems to have wished to exemplify the moral necessity of a due balance between our attention to the objects of our senses, and our meditation on the workings of our minds, – an *equilibrium* between the real and the imaginary worlds. In Hamlet this balance is disturbed: his thoughts, and the images of his fancy, are far more vivid than his actual perceptions, instantly passing through the *medium* of his contemplations, acquire, as they pass, a form and colour not naturally their own. Hence we see a great, an almost enormous, intellectual activity, and a proportionate aversion to real action ... The effect of this overbalance of the imaginative power is beautifully illustrated in the everlasting broodings and superfluous activities of Hamlet's mind, which, unseated from its healthy relation, is constantly occupied with the world within, and abstracted from the world without – giving substance to shadows, and throwing a mist over all commonplace actualities. (from *Lectures*, 1818)

I have smack of Hamlet myself, if I may say so. (from *Table Talk*, 24 June 1987)

A. C. BRADLEY

The *immediate* cause of [Hamlet's inaction] is simply that his habitual feeling is one of disgust at life and everything in it, himself included, – a disgust which varies in intensity, rising at times into a longing for death, sinking often into weary apathy, but is never dispelled for more than brief intervals. Such a state of feeling is inevitably adverse to *any* kind of decided action; the body is inert, the mind indifferent or worse; its response is, 'it does not matter', 'it is not worth while', 'it is no good'. And the action required of Hamlet is very exceptional. It is violent, dangerous, difficult to accomplish perfectly, on one side repulsive to a man of hounour and sensitive feeling, on another side involved in a certain mystery ... These obstacles would not suffice to prevent Hamlet from acting, if his state were normal; and against them there operate, even in morbid state, healthy and positive feelings, love of his father, loathing of his uncle, desire of revenge, desire to do duty. But the retarding motives acquire an unnatural strength because they have an ally in something far stronger than themselves, the melancholic disgust and apathy; while the healthy motives, emerging with difficulty from the central mass of diseased feeling, rapidly sink back into it and 'lose the name of action'.

(from *Shakespearean Tragedy*, 1904)

HELEN GARDNER

Although I have gone to the Elizabethans to ask how *Hamlet* first appeared to audiences which had applauded *The Spanish Tragedy* and *Titus Andronicus*, it is the moral uncertainties and the moral dilemmas of my own age which make me unable to see *Hamlet* in terms of the hero's failure or success in the task which the ghost lays upon him.

> For this same lord,
> I do repent; but heaven hath pleased it so,
> To punish me with this, and this with me,
> That I must be their scourge and minster.

Hamlet, speaking over the body of one of his victims, Polonius, speaks for all those called on to attempt to secure justice, the supporters of 'just wars' as well as those who fight in them. In trying to set *Hamlet* back into its own age, I seem to have found in it an image of my own time. The Elizabethan Hamlet assumes the look of the Hamlet of the Twentieth century. (from *The Business of Criticism*, 1959)

JAN KOTT

Hamlet was performed in Cracow in 1956 uniquivocally and with terrifying clarity. Doubtless it was a simplified *Hamlet*. But it is equally certain that this interpretation was so suggestive that when I reached for the text after the performance, I saw in it only a drama of political crime. To the classic question, whether Hamlet's madness is real or feigned, the Cracow production gave the following reply: Hamlet feigns madness, he puts on, in cold blood, a mask of madness in order to perform a *coup d'état*;

Hamlet is mad, because politics is itself madness when it destroys all feeling and affection.

I have nothing against such an interpretation. And I am not sorry for all the other Hamlets: for the moralist unable to draw a clear-cut line between good and evil; for the intellectual unable to find a sufficient reason for action; for the philosopher to whom the world's existence is a matter of doubt.

I prefer the youth deeply involved in politics, rid of illusions, sarcastic, passionate and brutal. A young rebel who has about him something of the charm of James Dean. His passion sometimes seems childish. No doubt he is more primitive than all previous Hamlets. Action, not reflection, is his forte. He is wild and drunk with indignation ... He does not yet experience deep moral doubts, but he is not a simpleton. He wants to know if his father has really been murdered. He cannot fully trust the Ghost, or any ghosts for that matter. He looks for more convincing evidence, and that is why he arranges a psychological test by staging the crime that has been committed. He loathes the world, and that is why he sacrifices Ophelia. But he does not flinch from a *coup d'état*. He knows, however, that a *coup* is a difficult affair. He considers all the pros and cons. He is a born conspirator. 'To be' means for him to revenge his father and to assassinate the king; while 'not to be' means to give up the fight.

... *Hamlet* is like a sponge. Unless produced in a stylized or antiquarian fashion, it immediately absorbs all the problems of out time.

(from *Shakespeare our Contemporary*, 1964)

Notes

Chapter One: History and Myth (Pages 1–18)

1 Charles Dickens, *Great Expectations*, 1860, ch. 31.
2 Peter Hall, quoted in Charles Marowitz and Simon Trussler, *Theatre at Work*, London, Methuen, 1967, p. 146.
3 See Geoffrey Bullough, (ed.), *Narrative and Dramatic Sources of Shakespeare*, London, Routledge and Kegan Paul, 1973, pp. 60–80.
4 Thomas Lodge, *Wits Miserie*, 1596, sig. H4ᵛ.
5 See Bullough, *Op. cit.*, p. 70 and pp. 110–11.
6 *To Be or Not to Be*, dir. Ernst Lubitsch, United Artists, 1942; *To Be or Not to Be*, dir. Mel Brooks, Twentieth Century Fox, 1985.
7 Portrait of J. P. Kemble by Sir Thomas Lawrence (1801), in the Tate Gallery; Buzz Goodbody's *Hamlet* was performed at the Royal Shakespeare Theatre's Other Place studio from April 1975.
8 Frontispiece of Rowe edition of *Hamlet*, 1709.
9 Tony Richardson's production played at the Round House Theatre, London, from February 1969; his film version was produced by Woodfall Production Co., 1969.
10 *Hamlet*, dir. Laurence Olivier, Two Cities Film/ Olivier/ Rank, 1948.
11 This school production, performed in 1963 at a Northern Grammar School with few thespian pretensions, had a notable cast: Hamlet was played by Martin Potter, now a film and TV actor; Claudius by Bob Peck, prominent in the RSC; and various parts by John Bleadale, who acts for television. The play was directed by John Linstrum, who directed Cardiff's Sherman Theatre until his recent death. I appropriately enough played one of the dispensable duo Rosencrantz and Guildenstern, though I can't remember (and am unsure if I ever knew) which one.
12 See R. M. Frye, 'Ladies, Gentlemen and Skulls', *Shakespeare Quarterly*, 30, 1979.
13 Delmore Schwarz, 'Gold Morning, Sweet Prince', in Laurence Lerner, (ed.), *Shakespeare's Tragedies*, Harmondsworth, Penguin, 1963.

Chapter Two: Stage and Text (Pages 18–34)

1 Graham Holderness, *Shakespeare's History*, Dublin, Gill and Macmillan, 1985, p. 13.
2 Sketched by Johannes de Witt in 1596, copied by Arend van Buchell. Original in the Bibliotheek der Rijkuniversiteit, Utrecht.
3 See Andrew Gurr, *The Shakespearean Stage, 1574–1642*, Cambridge, C.U.P., 1980, p. 125.
4 *Hamlet: First Quarto, 1603*, Menston, The Scholar press, 1969, G2.
5 See Robert Weimann, *Shakespeare and the Popular Tradition in the Theatre*, trans. Robert Schwarz, Baltimore, Johns Hopkins University Press, 1978.
6 See for example John Russel Brown, *Free Shakespeare*, London, Heinemann, 1974, pp. 111–2.
7 For example S. L. Bethell, *Shakespeare and the Popular Dramatic Tradition*, 1944, reprinted New York, Octagon Books, 1979.
8 See Alan C. Dessen, *Elizabethan Stage Conventions and Modern Interpreters*, Cambridge, C.U.P., 1984.
9 Bertolt Brecht, *The Messingkauf Dialogues*, trans. John Willett, Eyre Methuen, 1965, quotation from p. 59.
10 *Hamlet; the Text of the First Folio, 1623*, Menston, The Scholar Press, 1969, p. 47; *Hamlet: First Quarto*, D3.
11 Philip Edwards,'Introduction' to New Cambridge Shakespeare *Hamlet*, p. 9.
12 *Folio*, p. 102; *First Quarto*, I3.
13 Matthew Arnold, 'The Study of Poetry', *Essays in Criticism: Second Series*, London, Macmillan, 1889.
14 *Folio*, p. 102.
15 Edwards, *Op. cit.*, p. 8.

Chapter Three: Psychology of Revenge (Pages 34–57)

1 Despite the powerful emotional taboos that collect around the subject of incest, like all other crimes it is subject to social definition, and different societies draw the limits of sexual relationships in different ways. Today incest is concerned only with consanguinuity: but the view that no one should marry two siblings was still being argued in the nineteenth century. The ghost may therefore be defining Gertrude's crime quite precisely. On the other hand, he also accuses her of 'adultery': which must mean an accusation of infidelity while he was still alive. We can read this language either as the terms of Gertrude's particular guilt; or as the terms of the ghost's bitter and resentful anger.
2 T. S. Eliot, 'Hamlet', *Selected Essays,* London, Faber and Faber, 1932, p. 145.

3 Ernest Jones's study first appeared in the *American Journal of Psychology*, 1910, and was issued as a book *Hamlet and Oedipus* in 1949. Here Jones is quoted from Laurence Lerner, (ed.), *Shakespeare's Tragedies: an Anthology of Modern Criticism*, Harmondsworth, Penguin, 1968.

4 Jacques Lacan, 'Desire and the Interpretation of Desire in *Hamlet*', in Shoshona Feldman, *Literature and Psychoanalysis, the Question of Reading: Otherwise*, Baltimore, Johns Hopkins University Press, 1982.

5 A parallel structure can be found in other Shakespearean tragedies: in *Macbeth* the rebellion of Macdonwald and the Norwegian invasion of Sweno are far more easily suppressed than the internal threat to the state of Scotland represented by Macbeth himself; and in *Othello* we find a similarly decisive deflection of an enemy at the gates (the Turkish attack on Cyprus) which does nothing to suppress the far greater peril of the enemy within – Othello's jealousy. See *Macbeth*, 1.2 and *Othello*, 3.1.

6 Raymond Williams, *Keywords*, London, Fontana, 1975, pp. 184–9.

7 For a thorough review of this debate, and for further references, see Eleanor Prosser, *Revenge in Hamlet*, Stanford, Stanford University Press, 1967.

8 See Prosser, *Revenge*, pp. 3–35.

9 *Ibid.*, p. 5.

10 *Ibid.*, p. 7.

11 Francis Bacon, 'Of Revenge', (1625) in A. S. Gaye, (ed.), *the Essays of Francis Bacon*, Oxford, Claredon Press, 1911, pp. 27–9.

12 G. Wilson Knight, *The Wheel of Fire*, 1930; quoted from John Jump, (ed.), *Shakespeare: Hamlet, A Casebook*, London, Macmillan, 1968, p. 40.

13 See Lawrence Stone, *The Crisis of the Aristocracy 1558–1641*, Oxford, O.U.P., 1965.

Chapter Four: Madness and Metadrama (Pages 57–81)

1 *Hamlet, Second Quarto*, Menston, The Scolar Press, 1972, G2.

2 See, for example, Philip Edwards, *Op cit.*, p. 141.

3 *Second Quarto*, G.

4 J. Dover Wilson, for example, in *What Happens in Hamlet*, Cambridge, C.U.P., 1935; and Eleanor Prosser, *Revenge in Hamlet*, Stanford, Stanford University Press, 1967. For the ghost as the symbol of a radical indeterminancy in the play, see Terence Hawkes, *That Shakespehearian Rag*, London, Methuen, 1986.

5 See Bertolt Brecht, *The Messingkauf Dialogues*, trans. John Willett, London, Eyre Methuen, 1965, pp. 51–7.

6 L. C. Knights, *Hamlet and other Shakespearean Essays*, Cambridge, C.U.P., 1979, p. 56.

7   See Brecht, *Messingkauf Dialogues*; Walter Benjamin, *Illuminations*, London, Fontana, 1973; and Further Reading.

8   John Holloway, *The Story of the Night*, London, Routledge and Kegan Paul, 1961; quoted from John Jump, (ed), *Shakespeare: Hamlet, A Casebook*, London, Macmillan, 1968, pp. 161 and 163.

9   Maynard Mack, 'The World of *Hamlet*', *Yale Review*, xli, 1952; quoted from Jump, *Casebook* pp. 90–4 *passim*.

10 Sir Philip Sidney, *A Defence of Poetry*, ed. Jan van Dorsten, Oxford, O.U.P. 1966, pp. 65 and 67.

11 J. Dover Wilson, *What Happens*; quoted from Jump, *Casebook,* pp. 44–5.

12 *First Folio*, p. 58.

13 John Dover Wilson, (ed.), *Hamlet*, Cambridge, Cambridge University Press, 1934, 1958, (3.2.264–9).

14 *Hamlet, Prince of Denmark*, Royal Shakespeare Theatre, from 25 June 1980; dir. John Barton.

15 Anne Righter, *Shakespeare and the Idea of the Play*, Harmondsworth, Penguin, 1962.

16 RSC programme, 1980, quotes from Anne Barton, Introduction to her edition of *Hamlet* for the New Penguin Shakespeare, Harmondsworth, Penguin, 1980.

17 Anne Barton, Introduction *Op. Cit.*, p. 48.

18 Michael L. Greenwald, 'The Marriage of True Minds: the Bartons and *Hamlet*, 1980–1', in *Deutsche Shakespeare Gesellschaft West Jahrbuch*, 1983, p. 156.

Chapter Five: Catharsis or Catastrophe? (Pages 81–102)

1   Brecht, *Messingkauf Dialogues*, p. 60.

2   I am indebted to John Turner, who sees Hamlet and Claudius as the 'mighty opposites' of Renaissance ideology, the idealist and the machievel, for this and many other ideas embodied in this text (see Further Reading).

3   Terry Eagleton, *William Shakespeare,* Oxford, Blackwell.

4   *Ibid.*, p. 7.

5   See also Terry Hawkes, '*Hamlet*: the play on words', in *Shakespeare's Talking Animals*, London, Edward Arnold, 1973.

6   Walter Benjamin, *Illuminations*, London, Fontana, 1973, p. 259.

7   One of the best examples of such critical procedure is Elaine Showalter's 'Representing Ophelia: women, madness and the responsibilities of feminist criticism', in Patricia Parker and Geoffrey Hartmann, (eds.), *Shakespeare and the Question of Theory*, London, Methuen, 1986. Also see Further Reading.

8   Sir Philip Sidney: *The Defence of Poetry*, 1576, (ed.) Jan van Dorsten, Oxford, O.U.P. 1966, p. 67.

9   An aspect amusingly burlesqued in a parody called 'The Skinhead

Hamlet' in *The Faber Book of Literary Parodies*, London, Faber and Faber, 1900:

GERTRUDE: There is a willow grows aslant a brook –
LAERTES: Get on with it, slag!
GERTRUDE: Ophelia's fucking drowned!

10 Philip Edwards, (ed.), *The New Cambridge Shakespeare: Hamlet*, Cambridge, C.U.P., 1985, p. 32.
11 See Jan Kott, *Shakespeare our Contemporary*, London, Methuen, 1964.
12 Substantial portions of the 'Osric' scene are to be found in the Second Quarto, but not in the Folio text: one indication of a possible playhouse cut.
13 Holloway, quoted from Jump, *Casebook*, p. 171.
14 Longer extracts from each of the following sources can be found in Jump, *Casebook*, pp. 30–1, 38–9, 137–50, 196–209.

Suggestions for further reading

Chapter 1
The best modern editions of *Hamlet* are the recommended text, the *New Cambridge Shakespeare*, (ed.) Philip Edwards, Cambridge, C.U.P., 1985; and the *Arden Shakespeare,* (ed.) Harold Jenkins, London, Methuen, 1982. The *New Penguin Shakespeare,* (ed.) T.J.B. Spencer, Harmondsworth, Penguin, 1980, is an adequate edition: but older editions such as that of J. Dover Wilson (*The New Shakespeare*, Cambridge, C.U.P., 1934) can be unreliable and misleading. Good editions carry textual variants, but the best way of appreciating the radical divergences between Quarto and Folio texts is to read them comparatively: see *Hamlet; the Text of the First Folio, 1623*, Menston, The Scolar Press, 1969; *Hamlet: First Quarto, 1603*,

Menston, The Scolar Press, 1969; *and Hamlet: Second Quarto,* Menston, The Scolar Press, 1972.

Many of the issues raised and discussed in this chapter are further developed in a critical anthology *The Shakespeare Myth,* (ed.) Graham Holderness, Manchester, M.U.P., 1987. The presence of Shakespeare in contemporary media and in advertising is discussed there by Derek Longhurst, in ' "You base football player!": Shakespeare in contemporary popular culture'; and the nature of Shakespeare's 'universality' by Alan Sinfield, 'Making Space: appropriation and confrontation in recent British plays'. The problems of 'authorship' in relation to Shakespeare are explored in the same volume by Graham Holderness, 'Bardolotry: or the cultural materialist's guide to Stratford-upon-Avon', and by John Drakakis, 'Theatre, Ideology and Institution: Shakespeare and the roadsweepers'. A brilliant analysis of Shakespearean 'authorship' is to be found in Terry Hawkes, *That Shakespeherian Rag,* London, Methuen, 1986, pp. 75–6; and a theoretical exposition of the general concept in Michel Foucault, *Language, Counter-Memory, Practice,* Oxford, Blackwell, 1977.

Some indication of the variety of possible methods for presenting *Hamlet* can be found in Ralph Berry, *Changing Styles in Shakespeare,* London, George Allen and Unwin, 1981; and an illustrated historical account of production in Herbert Marshall, (ed.) *Hamlet Through the Ages: a pictoral record from 1709,* London, Rockliff Publishing Company, 1952. Buzz Goodbody's remarkable production is chronicled in Colin Chambers, *Other Spaces,* London, Eyre Methuen and TQ Productions, 1980. Both the Tony Richardson and Laurence Olivier films are discussed in Roger Manvell, *Shakespeare and the Film,* South Brunswick and New York: A. S. Barnes and Co., 1971, and in Jack Jorgens, *Shakespeare on Film,* Bloomington, Indiana University Press, 1977.

Chapter 2

The best short introductions to the Elizabethan theatre are Andrew Gurr, *The Shakespearean Stage, 1574–1642,* Cambridge, C.U.P., 2nd edition, 1980; and Peter Thomson, *Shakespeare's Theatre,* London, Routledge and Kegan Paul, 1983. Both these studies draw on larger scholarly works: Glynne Wickham's *Early English Stages, 1300–1600,* vol. 2, 1576–1660, London, Routledge and Kegan Paul, 1972; and beyond that, E. K. Chambers' monumental *The Elizabethan Stage,* Oxford, The Clarendon Press, 1923. For a theoretical discussion of the underlying social and cultural relationships see Graham Holderness, *Shakespeare's History,* Dublin, Gill and Macmillan, 1985. C. Walter Hodges' visual reconstructions of the Shakespearean theatre can be found in his *The Globe Restored: a study of the Elizabethan theatre,* London, Ernest Benn, 1953. Robert Weimann's study of the social and cultural significance of theatrical spaces and conventions – *Shakespeare and the Popular Tradition in the Theatre*, trans. Robert Schwarz, Baltimore, Johns Hopkins University Press, 1978, can be strongly recommended; and Professor Weimann has applied these methods to *Hamlet* in 'Hamlet and mimesis', in Patricia Parker and Geoffrey Hartmann, (eds.), *Shakespeare and the Question of Theory*, London: Methuen, 1986.

For some of the various different conclusions it is possible to draw from what evidence there is, about the physical shape of the Elizabethan theatres, see Thomson, *Shakespeare's Theatre* (1983), and John Russel Brown, *Free Shakespeare*, London, Heinemann, 1974, and *Discovering Shakespeare's Plays*, Macmillan, 1981; S. L. Bethell, *Shakespeare and the Popular Dramatic Tradition*, 1944, reprinted New York, Octagon Books, 1970, and Terry Hawkes, *Shakespeare's Talking Animals*, London, Methuen, 1973; Alan C. Dessen, *Elizabethan Stage Conventions and Modern Interpreters*, Cambridge, C.U.P., 1984, supplemented by Dessen's 'Shakespeare and the theatrical conventions of his time', in Stanley Wells, (ed.), *The Cambridge Companion to Shakespeare Studies*, Cambridge, C.U.P., 1986, and Gary Taylor, 'Introduction' to his edition of *Henry V*, (The New Oxford Shakespeare), Oxford, O.U.P., 1982; Bertolt Brecht, *The Messingkauf Dialogues*, trans. John Willett, Eyre Methuen, 1965, and Holderness, *Shakespeare's History* (1985) and '*Romeo and Juliet*: Empathy and Alienation', *Shakespeare Jahrbuch*, 1987.

For an introduction to textual scholarship see E. A. J. Honigmann, *The Stability of Shakespeare's Text*, London, Edward Arnold, 1965; Stanley Wells, *Re-editing Shakespeare for the Modern Reader*, Oxford, O.U.P., 1984; and MacD. P. Jackson, 'The transmission of Shakespeare's text', in Wells (ed.), *The Cambridge Companion* (1986).

Chapter 3

Claudius and Hamlet are regarded as 'mighty opposites' in Terry Hawkes's 'Telmah', in *That Shakespeherian Rag*, (1986), and in an as yet unpublished essay on *Hamlet* by John Turner, to which this entire text is deeply indebted, and which should be appearing in a study of Shakespeare and the Renaissance court, to be published by Macmillan. The historicist qualities of the play are discussed by the late Arnold Kettle in 'From *Hamlet* to *Lear*', in his edition *Shakespeare in a Changing World*, London, Lawrence and Wishart, 1964; a different historicist view is offered by Jan Kott in *Shakespeare Our Contemporary*, London, Methuen, 1964; and there are some very interesting pages on *Hamlet* linking history and psychology in D. H. Lawrence's *Twilight in Italy*, (1916), Harmondsworth, Penguin, 1960. The politics and languages of the Danish court are ably discussed by Terry Eagleton in *Shakespeare and Society*,

London, Chatto and Windus, 1967. An earlier view of Hamlet as morbid and psychologically disturbed can be found in G. Wilson Knight, *The Wheel of Fire*, Oxford, O.U.P., 1930; and in L. C. Knight's, *Hamlet and Other Shakespearean Essays,* Cambridge, C.U.P., 1979.

The Freudian reading of *Hamlet* can be represented by the extracts from Ernest Jones's and T. S. Eliot's essays reprinted in John Jump, (ed.), *Shakespeare: Hamlet, A Casebook,* London, Macmillan, 1968; and the neo-Freudian reading of Jacques Lacan in his 'Desire and the Interpretation of Desire in *Hamlet*', in Shoshona Feldman, (ed.), *Literature and Psychoanalysis: the Question of Reading: Otherwise,* Baltimore, Johns Hopkins University Press, 1982.

The importance of social 'bonds' is a recurrent theme througout Graham Holderness *et al.*, *The Play of History: studies in the Renaissance Historical Imagination,* London, Macmillan (Contemporary Interpretations of Shakespeare), 1987; and the vocabulary of 'nature' thoroughly discussed in J. F. Danby's *Shakespeare's Doctrine of Nature*, London, Faber and Faber, 1949. Eleanor Prosser, *Revenge in Hamlet*, Stanford, Stanford University Press, 1967, is an adequate source, with abundant further references, for the revenge convention; and a study linking revenge with theatricality is P. Mercer's *Hamlet and the Acting of Revenge,* London, Macmillan (Contemporary Interpretations of Shakespeare), 1987.

The movement from a criticism concerned to locate Hamlet's 'delay' in his character to a criticism more conscious of obstacle and difficulty, can be traced from Goethe, Schlegel and Coleridge (represented in Jump, *A Casebook*, (1968)), through A. C. Bradley, *Shakespearean Tragedy*, London, Macmillan, 1904, to J. Dover Wilson, *What Happens in Hamlet,* Cambridge, C.U.P., 1935, to Hawkes, *That Shakespeherian Rag*, (1986).

Chapter 4

Robert Weimann's *Shakespeare and the Popular Tradition*, (1978), and '*Hamlet and Mimesis*' (1986), contain extended discussions of the relations between verse and prose, and between illusionistic and self-reflexive stage positions. For metadrama, see (with particular emphasis on *Hamlet*), James L. Calderwood, *To Be and Not to Be: Negation and Metadrama in Hamlet,* New York, 1983; and Sidney Homan, *When the Theatre Turns to Itself*, Lewisburg, Bucknell University Press, London and Toronto, Associated University Presses, 1981; and for more general considerations Anne Righter, *Shakespeare and the Idea of the Play*, (1962), Harmondsworth, Penguin, 1967, and James L. Calderwood, *Shakespearean Metadrama*, Minneapolis, 1971.

Chapter 5

Post-structuralist readings of *Hamlet* can be found in Hawkes, *Shakespeare's Talking Animals*, (1973), and *That Shakespeherian Rag*, (1986); and a general post-structuralist account of Shakespeare in Terry Eagleton, *William Shakespeare*, Oxford, Basil Blackwell, 1986. For feminist criticism, Elaine Showalter's 'Representing Ophelia: women, madness and the responsibilities of feminist criticism', in Parker and Hartmann, (eds.), *Question of Theory*, (1986), contains an excellent bibliography; and see also Jacqueline Rose, 'Sexuality in the Reading of Shakespeare', in John Drakakis, (ed.), *Alternative Shakespeares,* London, Methuen, 1986. A comprehensive review of feminist Shakespeare criticism is to be found in Ann Thompson, '"The warrant of womanhood": Shakespeare and Feminist Criticism' in Holderness, (ed.), *The Shakespeare Myth* (1987). Romantic criticism can be sampled in the first part of Jump, (ed.), *A Casebook* (1968).

Index